ASPECTS
OF
TOLERATION

ASPECTS

OF

TOLERATION

PHILOSOPHICAL STUDIES

Edited by

JOHN HORTON &
SUSAN MENDUS

Methuen
London and New York

First published in 1985 by
Methuen & Co. Ltd
11 New Fetter Lane, London EC4P 4EE

Published in the USA by
Methuen & Co.
in association with Methuen, Inc.
29 West 35th Street, New York, NY 10001

Printed in Great Britain at the University Press, Cambridge
Filmset by Northumberland Press Ltd,
Gateshead, Tyne and Wear

British Library Cataloguing in Publication Data

Aspects of toleration.
1. Toleration
I. Horton, John   II. Mendus, Susan
179'.9   BJ1431

ISBN 0-416-39290-3

Library of Congress Cataloging in Publication Data
Main entry under title:

Aspects of toleration.

Includes index.
Contents: Introduction/John Horton and Susan Mendus—Toleration,
individual differences and respect for persons/Albert Weale—Toleration and
right to freedom/Thomas Baldwin—[etc.]

1. Toleration—Addresses, Essays, Lectures
I. Horton, John (John P.)   II. Mendus, Susan
BJ1431.A86   1985
179'.9   85-13656

ISBN 0-416-39290-3

Contents

Preface

All the essays in this volume arose from a programme of studies concerned with philosophical and theoretical aspects of toleration, initiated and supported by the C. and J. B. Morrell Trust, based at the University of York. The Trust supports an annual lecture given by a person of international repute, a postgraduate course on political philosophy with special reference to toleration (financing five annual studentships), a research fellow, an annual conference and a regular series of seminars attended by interested members of the Politics and Philosophy Departments at York. The essays in this volume, with one exception, were originally presented as papers to the previously mentioned seminars and benefited from their discussion in those meetings. The one exception, the essay by Peter Jones, was presented at the first annual Toleration Conference in 1983 and seemed especially appropriate to be included in this volume. Peter Jones, a lecturer in the Department of Politics at the University of Newcastle, is the only contributor who was not a member of either the Politics or Philosophy Departments of the University of York. Thomas Baldwin has subsequently moved to the University of Cambridge.

Our principal acknowledgement is of course to the Trustees of the C. and J. B. Morrell Trust, both for their general support of the study of toleration and in particular for their generous financial and other assistance towards the publication of this book. All the contributors have been helpful but we would especially like to thank David Edwards, Peter Nicholson and Albert Weale for their advice and suggestions. We have also been very fortunate that Methuen chose as an external referee Professor David Raphael, who has taken an exceptionally conscientious and constructive interest in the book's progress. Another, anonymous, referee also made some useful suggestions. The manuscript was typed most efficiently by Sally Baker, Sally Cuthbert, Barbara Dodds, Kathleen Hunter, Barbara Olive and Dorothy Skidmore. Jo Guise and Dorothy Skidmore also provided valuable administrative assistance and Lynne Horton helped with proofreading. Finally, Nancy Marten has been as sympathetic and helpful an editor as we could hope to have had.

Introduction

JOHN HORTON AND SUSAN MENDUS

The essays in this volume are concerned with the theoretical and conceptual issues involved in the idea of toleration. They discuss these issues primarily in the context of contemporary debates about racial, religious and sexual toleration. However, in considering these problems, the contributors often refer to and draw upon the work of earlier philosophers and political theorists. In particular, John Stuart Mill's essay *On Liberty* is a frequent point of reference and it is this work that provides the theoretical context for much contemporary writing on toleration.[1] However, Mill's work itself is the culmination of over three hundred years of discussion and debate about the place of toleration in the modern state of Western Europe and, more latterly, North America. In this introduction we shall first very briefly indicate some of the main developments in ideas about toleration with especial emphasis on Mill's seminal essay; we will then consider the three main areas of practical concern with which the essays in this collection deal; and finally we will identify what we take to be some of the most significant theoretical issues which are relevant to those practical problems and which the essays in this volume explore.

★

Many of the most powerful and lasting arguments for toleration have their roots in the religious controversies and struggles, originating with the Reformation, which divided Europe in the sixteenth and seventeenth centuries. Early formulations and defences of the idea of toleration were often developed to cope with the fierce religious differences which were a continuing threat to civil order and personal security. Some of these arguments were highly historically specific and closely bound up with complex theological positions which are of little contemporary relevance. Other arguments though more general were of an essentially pragmatic nature, being concerned with the most feasible means of avoiding civil disorder. These often remain relevant and are sometimes invoked in current discussions but they are of only limited theoretical interest. There were, however, at least two kinds of argument which have proved to be of continuing practical relevance and of considerable theoretical interest. These arguments are developed in different ways and to different degrees by many of the major theorists of toleration such as Althusius, Milton, Spinoza, Pufendorf and perhaps most famously Locke in his *A Letter on Toleration*. Since a genuine historical account of emerging ideas about toleration is not possible here we shall merely introduce these two arguments in general terms as a prelude to a rather fuller discussion of *On Liberty*.[2]

The first argument, which has its roots in Protestant theology but is of more general import, justifies toleration in terms of the claims of conscience. One aspect of this argument is that the nature of conscience is such that it cannot be subjected to effective external coercion. Thus while behaviour may be directly controlled, what a person genuinely thinks and believes is largely inaccessible to the potential coercer. The other more important aspect of this argument lay in the claim that the value or worth of what is believed, and in some cases practised, is dependent upon the way in which such beliefs came to be held. For example, one of Milton's arguments for the toleration and free expression of a wide (though limited) range of opinions advanced in his *Areopagitica* was that a person was only truly virtuous where virtue was freely chosen in preference to, and with full knowledge of the wicked and evil.[3] Spinoza too built such claims into the political philosophy of his *Tractatus Theologico-Politicus*[4] and of course similar arguments were to be fundamental to Mill's case in *On Liberty*.

The second argument for toleration was associated with the increasing separation of Church and State and the corresponding functions thought appropriate to each. Of especial importance was the idea that the role of the state, and hence of coercive power, was

2

to maintain civil order rather than impose preferred creeds or faiths upon its subjects. The spiritual well-being of the person remained the legitimate concern of the Church, but a Church shorn of coercive power. Thus Locke[5] argued that toleration should extend to all beliefs and practices that do not represent a threat to public order and government authority. His view that Catholics owed allegiance to a foreign power, the Pope, and that atheists could not be trusted because they recognized no divine sanction to support their oaths, accounted for his refusal to extend toleration to these two groups. However, the importance of Locke's claims for the development of the idea of toleration lay less in these exclusions than in the general nature of the argument. For with this argument can be seen the germination of the idea that there are some areas of individual activity in which it is simply not the business of the state to prescribe or legislate unless they pose a serious threat to the security of the state. Again it can be seen that there is an affinity between this argument and another of the central claims of *On Liberty*.

John Stuart Mill's essay *On Liberty* was first published in 1859. In the opening chapter of the essay Mill declares that his aim is to defend 'one very simple principle'. That principle is that

> the sole end for which mankind are warranted, individually or collectively, in interfering with the liberty of action of any of their number, is self-protection. That the only purpose for which power can be rightfully exercised over any member of a civilised community, against his will, is to prevent harm to others. His own good, either physical or moral, is not a sufficient warrant. He cannot rightfully be compelled to do or forbear because it will be better for him to do so, because it will make him happier, because, in the opinions of others, to do so would be wise, or even right. These are good reasons for remonstrating with him, or reasoning with him, or persuading him, or entreating him, but not for compelling him, or visiting him with any evil in case he do otherwise. To justify that, the conduct from which it is desired to deter him, must be calculated to produce evil to some one else. The only part of the conduct of any one, for which he is amenable to society, is that which concerns others. In the part which merely concerns himself, his

3

independence is, of right, absolute. Over himself, over his own body and mind, the individual is sovereign.[6]

It is difficult to exaggerate the importance of the principle of *On Liberty*, which has had enormous influence on philosophical, political and legal thinkers and is still recognized today as a landmark in the history of liberalism. However, the apparently 'very simple principle' which Mill advanced has proved far from simple either in interpretation or in application. In this introduction we can only point to three areas of difficulty and say something about each in turn. These three areas are: Mill's concept of harm, his distinction between self-regarding and other-regarding action, and his defence of free speech. However, we should make it clear that our purpose in rehearsing these difficulties is not to undermine the value of Mill's *Essay* nor to suggest that possible resolutions of them may not be reconstructed from his work. Rather we wish to suggest some of the most important questions which any account of toleration will need to answer. It is the great virtue of *On Liberty* that it raises most of these questions in an acute and pressing form.

In the statement of the principle of *On Liberty* Mill insists that coercion may justifiably be employed only to prevent harm to others. In making this claim Mill seems to assume that the concept of harm will provide a fairly clear and straightforward criterion for assessing whether or not legislation might be legitimate and proper. It is far from obvious, however, that this assumption is justified. It may be argued against Mill that the term 'harm' is itself value-laden, and that there can be no general agreement about whether something constitutes a harm except against the background of a shared morality. Even if *physical* harm were thought to be uncontroversial, there is no reason to think that it is either the only possible harm or necessarily the most serious of harms. Even a cursory consideration of practices such as suttee, female circumcision, blood transfusions or the engagement in unconventional sexual practices shows how diverse are the views about whether, and to what extent, these activities may be considered harmful. This then is the first difficulty inherent in Mill's principle. A second problem arises from the attempt to draw a clear distinction between self-regarding and other-regarding action; for Mill's claim that coercion may be employed only to prevent harm *to others* depends upon the plausibility of that distinction. However it has been argued by his critics that there is no clearly identifiable realm of self-regarding actions, or at least in so far as there is it will include only the most trivial actions, for man is essentially a social being and nearly all his acts have consequences for others. It seems clear that Mill would not wish his principle to be interpreted so as to allow only the most trivial or banal of actions to count as self-regarding, yet it is not obvious how he can make the principle do the work he requires of it without some fuller explanation of the self-regarding/other-regarding distinction. The literature on this topic is enormous, and this is not the place to engage in detailed textual criticism of Mill's principle, but it is worth noting that much recent scholarship has been concerned to defend Mill on this point.[7]

Whatever its merits, however, it is important not to underestimate the influence of Mill's line of argument on subsequent liberal thought. To take only one example, though a particularly famous one, Mill's distinction between self-regarding and other-regarding conduct has had important repercussions for modern legal theory and practice. In 1957 the *Report of the Committee on Homosexual Offences and Prostitution*, generally known as the Wolfenden Report, advocated, amongst other things, that 'homosexual behaviour between consenting adults in private should no longer be a criminal offence'. The Committee's grounds were that 'it is not, in our view, the function of the law to intervene in the private lives of citizens, or to seek to enforce any particular pattern of behaviour'.[8] The spirit of *On Liberty* is clearly seen in this statement of principle, and in the subsequent recommendations which included revisions of the law concerning prostitution as well as that concerning homosexuality. The Report, however, sparked off an important controversy in which Lord Devlin argued against the Committee and its defender, Professor H. L. A. Hart, that there can be no clearly defined sphere of self-regarding actions, actions which affect only the private lives of citizens.[9] 'You may argue,' said Devlin, 'that if a man's sins affect only himself, it cannot be the concern of society. If he chooses to get drunk every night in the privacy of his own home, is anyone except himself the worse for it? But suppose a quarter or a half of the population got drunk

5

every night, what sort of society would it be?'[10] Lord Devlin's argument combines the denial of a clear self-regarding/other-regarding distinction with an affirmation of the justifiability of what has been called 'legal moralism'. Against many liberals he urges that the enforcement of particular standards of moral behaviour may be the proper business of the law. Indeed, he goes so far as to say that the enforcement of society's shared morality is a 'vital function' of the law, and thus he challenges Mill and his modern-day counterparts to justify their claim that there is a sphere of self-regarding actions distinct from other-regarding behaviour and that it is improper for the law to intervene in the self-regarding sphere.

The final aspect of Mill's *On Liberty* which is pertinent here is his defence of freedom of expression. Mill considers it 'imperative that human beings should be free to form opinions, and to express their opinions without reserve'.[11] This is not, however, tantamount to a claim that every man should be free to act on his opinions, for 'No one pretends that acts should be as free as opinions.'[12] Moreover, Mill allows for an apparent exception to the principle of free expression when he writes:

> An opinion that corn-dealers are starvers of the poor, or that private property is robbery, ought to be unmolested when simply circulated through the press, but may justly incur punishment when delivered orally to an excited mob assembled before the house of a corn-dealer, or when handed about among the same mob in the form of a placard.[13]

What is important here is the fact that Mill isolates two crucial, yet problematic features of liberal thought: firstly, the powerful presumption in favour of freedom of speech, going far beyond the freedom allowed to actions; secondly, the difficulty of drawing a clear distinction between opinions and actions, and in particular between the legitimate expression of opinions and 'rabble rousing' or 'incitement to violence'. Yet we need to know why the expression of opinion should warrant this privileged position, and also what the justification is of the limits set upon that freedom by, for example, libel and slander laws and laws prohibiting incitement to racial hatred. While Mill gives considerable attention to the first of these questions, the second is largely ignored in *On Liberty*.

These three areas of Mill's argument in *On Liberty* – the concept of harm; the self-regarding/other-regarding distinction; and the defence of free speech – highlight some of the theoretical problems associated with the general topic of toleration and we shall say a little more about three of these later. However, before doing so we shall briefly indicate the main areas of social life in Britain in which the question of toleration has been especially pressing in recent decades.

★

On Liberty, though remaining probably the most fruitful source for ideas about the nature and value of toleration, was written in the mid-nineteenth century, a time in many respects different from our own. In recent years the need for a coherent analysis of the concept of toleration has become pressing not least because of social and political changes within our society. The theoretical and philosophical issues have assumed great importance precisely because of the urgent need to answer practical questions. As Britain has developed into a multi-cultural and multi-racial society, so the need to define the scope and limits of racial and religious toleration has grown. Similarly, the widespread liberalism with regard to sexual mores of the 1960s and early 1970s is now being challenged by some feminist and religious groups, which urge greater restriction of obscene and pornographic material and more stringent punishment for sexual offenders. The practical difficulties of racial, religious and sexual toleration thus highlight the need for a careful philosophical analysis of toleration. In this section we shall say something about each of these three areas of practical concern and in the next go on to indicate three particularly important theoretical issues concerning toleration which are taken up in the essays in this volume.

Sexual toleration

A crucial watershed in the liberalizing of British law governing sexual morality occurred in 1967 with the passing of the Sexual Offences Act. This Act decriminalized homosexuality between consenting male adults in private and in so doing officially endorsed the recommendations of the Wolfenden Committee.

The importance of the Wolfenden Committee's recommendation lies in its insistence on a clear distinction between crime and sin, and in its assertion that sin – private immorality – is not the business of the law. Private immorality must be tolerated. Nevertheless, the toleration of private immorality should not extend to 'activities which offend against public order and decency or expose the ordinary citizen to what is offensive or injurious'. The term 'injurious' in this context, and in British law generally, covers both physical and moral injury, and the belief that there can be such a thing as moral injury, or moral harm is embodied in the 1959 Obscene Publications Act. According to that Act an article is obscene if 'its effect ... is such as to tend to deprave and corrupt persons who are likely ... to read see or hear the matter contained or embodied in it'.[14] Thus, while the Wolfenden Committee held that 'it is not the duty of the law to concern itself with immorality as such', the Obscene Publications Act clearly implies both that there is such a thing as moral harm and that it is the proper business of the law to protect individuals against such harm. The problem here of course is exactly that which faces Mill's principle: what is the precise scope of the term 'harm' and how are we to identify moral harms? In 1979 the *Report of the Committee on Obscenity and Film Censorship*, the Williams Committee, pointed to just these difficulties in interpreting and applying the Obscene Publications Act. Scepticism about the possibility of identifying moral harms, coupled with a belief in the overriding importance of free speech, led to their proposals for liberalizing the law governing obscene publications.[15] However, their proposals have not yet been implemented and the recent 'Bright Bill', primarily aimed at restricting the sale and showing of so-called 'video nasties', suggests that the tide towards greater toleration is at least temporarily on the turn and that the belief in the possibility of moral harm runs very deep, even if we are little further advanced than Mill in specifying the exact scope and nature of moral harm.

Religious toleration

The demand for reform of laws governing sexual morality and obscene publications has not, however, been paralleled by liberali-

8

zing moves in the area of religious toleration. The reason is quite simply that, until very recently, it was thought that nothing needed to be done. As long ago as 1949 Lord Denning felt able to claim that

> we have attained to as high, if not a higher degree of religious freedom than any other country ... the reason for this [blasphemy] law was because it was thought that a denial of Christianity was liable to shake the fabric of society, which was itself founded on the Christian religion. There is no such danger to society now and the offence of blasphemy is a dead letter.[16]

In 1977, however, the 'dead letter' was invoked when Mrs Mary Whitehouse appealed to the common law of blasphemy in a largely successful prosecution of the magazine *Gay News* and its editor, Denis Lemon, who had published a poem by James Kirkup entitled 'The Love that Dares to Speak its Name'. The charge against *Gay News* was that it had published 'a blasphemous libel concerning the Christian religion, namely an obscene poem and illustration vilifying Christ in his life and in his crucifixion'.[17] The trial and the verdict served to highlight the fact that British law, far from exemplifying religious tolerance, in fact protects only Christians. It is, of course, questionable whether any religion should be so protected by law, but if the law is to offer protection at all, why should it not extend its protection to all religious creeds and sects represented within society? This question is particularly pertinent in a society such as our own, which now contains representatives of many different faiths.

While concurring in the decision on the *Gay News* trial Lord Scarman remarked,

> In an increasingly plural society such as that of modern Britain it is necessary not only to respect the differing religious beliefs, feelings and practices of all but also to protect them from scurrility, vilification, ridicule and contempt ... My criticism of the common law offence of blasphemy is not that it exists but that it is not sufficiently comprehensive.[18]

In this judgment Lord Scarman points to two theoretical issues raised by the practical problems of religious toleration: firstly, whether it is justifiable to curb freedom of expression at all in order to protect the religious sentiments of members of society; secondly, whether the requirement to show equal respect for all persons, whatever their religious beliefs, demands an extension of the common law offence of blasphemy to cover other religions.[19] Related to these two questions are further problems. Firstly, why should *religious* belief be singled out as the proper object of legal protection rather than secular moral beliefs which may also be very deeply held? Secondly, how are genuine religions to be distinguished from pseudo-religious cults? This second problem is especially acute when faced with the claims to be religions of such groups as the 'Moonies' and 'Scientologists'.

Racial toleration

The pluralistic nature of contemporary Britain generates problems concerning racial as well as religious toleration: diversity of religious creeds is partly a function of diversity of race and culture and whilst the sensitivities of Muslims as a religious group may not be protected by law, the sensitivities of Muslims as a cultural group are, to some extent, protected by the Race Relations Act of 1965. Moreover, the 1976 Race Relations Act created a new offence of incitement to racial hatred and provides that a person commits an offence if 'he uses ... words which are threatening, abusive or insulting in a case where ... hatred is likely to be stirred up against any racial group'.[20] Here again, however, the requirement to show equal respect for all persons may be thought to conflict with the right to freedom of expression and organizations such as the National Front have challenged the 1976 Act, claiming it to be an attack on the right to free speech. In his book *The National Front* Nigel Fielding puts the matter neatly:

> The idea of free speech is a major component of liberal ideology, and is used by both extreme Left and extreme Right to justify political violence. The National Front's consistent line in the face of often violent confrontation is that they will not back down in their defence of free speech.[21]

Thus the requirements of racial toleration, the protection of racial groups from discrimination and abuse, may seriously conflict with many individual freedoms. It may be that tolerance and freedom are intimately connected, but how much toleration does freedom require, and at what point may we be free to be intolerant?

The three problem areas mentioned above – sexual, religious and racial toleration – indicate some of the difficulties involved in the practice of toleration. Most conspicuously they show how the requirements of toleration in different spheres may conflict and the complexity of the relationship between toleration and freedom. The papers in this volume refer to these three areas in the course of more general discussions about the nature of toleration and its relation to ideas of harm, freedom and respect for persons. Racial toleration and its relation to freedom is discussed by Alex Callinicos, while the relationship between freedom and toleration more generally is examined by Thomas Baldwin. Religious toleration is the theme of David Edwards's paper, while sexual toleration, in particular the toleration of obscene or pornographic material, is the subject of Susan Mendus's contribution. Peter Jones and John Horton are concerned with different aspects of the relationship between harm and toleration. The opening and concluding papers, by Albert Weale and Peter Nicholson respectively, provide overviews of the justification and meaning of toleration in a modern society such as our own.

*

So far we have concentrated on the practical issues with which the papers are concerned, but what of the theoretical problems to which they give rise? Broadly there seem to be three principal areas of theoretical interest – the relationship between toleration and harm; the relationship between toleration and freedom, particularly freedom of expression; and the relationship between toleration and the idea of respect for persons. We shall consider these in turn.

Toleration and harm

In stating his principle, quoted above, Mill provided a criterion for identifying the circumstances in which intolerance may be legitimate. If an action harms others, then it may be quite proper to prohibit it. If, on the other hand, an action does not harm others, then it must be tolerated. However, as John Horton points out in his contribution to this volume, if Mill's harm principle is to be effective there needs to be a relatively clear and commonly agreed understanding of what is harmful. This view is adopted more or less explicitly by many contemporary liberals, but Horton's argument is that what is harmful is itself a matter of dispute. He suggests that disagreements about whether something constitutes a harm will be most likely to occur where there are deep and serious differences of moral opinion. Furthermore, it is in just those circumstances that the problem of toleration is likely to be especially acute and thus 'harm' will not provide a neutral criterion for deciding whether or not an activity should be tolerated. Peter Jones tackles a different aspect of the harm principle in showing how it may pose a serious dilemma for the liberal. Standardly, liberalism resists paternalistic action or legislation, but sometimes apparently paternalistic behaviour may be justified by appeal to what Jones calls 'the moral effect' argument. This argument aims to show how apparently paternalistic action may have an 'other-regarding' justification. Thus, for example, legislation requiring the wearing of seat belts may be justified not because of any benefit accruing to the wearer, but because the injuries consequent upon not wearing a seat belt impose duties on others in society to bring aid to the injured. It is the burdensome nature of these duties, and not paternalism, which justifies the legislation but it is obvious that this justification for restricting activities may be used to pursue extremely illiberal and intolerant policies and is therefore likely to be unpopular with the liberal. However, some such justification can be dispensed with only at the cost of equity, for if one person is allowed to use his freedom recklessly and others then have to come to his aid, one person's freedom is being exercised at the expense of that of others. It is not clear how this problem would be resolved by the liberal. Susan Mendus's essay considers the application of the harm principle specifically to the question of the restriction of obscene or pornographic material. The Williams Committee asserts that pornography should be tolerated because and in so far as it cannot be shown to cause any identifiable harm. Mendus claims that some opponents of pornography, particularly some feminist critics, do not hold a causal thesis of the kind implied by Mill and employed by Williams. Rather, their claim is that

certain kinds of material are corrupt in themselves and independent of any further harm they may bring about. Thus Mendus and
Horton agree in their criticism of the common assumption that
toleration is required in cases in which no harm is done, by denying
that an independently specifiable and uncontroversial account of
harm can be given.

Toleration and freedom

The uneasy relationship between the requirements of toleration
and the requirements of freedom of opinion and expression is
thrown into relief by considering the National Front's opposition
to the Race Relations Act. It is also discussed in two of the essays
printed here. Thomas Baldwin urges that the duty to tolerate rests
upon a right to freedom and that it is this which explains why
toleration may be not merely prudent, but morally obligatory.
Furthermore the justification of toleration in terms of a right to
freedom not only requires toleration of dissentient views and
opinions but will establish the limits of such toleration. Alex
Callinicos takes up this latter point, for while recognizing the
relationship between toleration and freedom, he is also anxious to
define the limits of toleration. Though largely critical of Marcuse's
idea of 'repressive tolerance', he agrees that toleration need not
extend to the activities of fascist groups such as the National Front,
in the propagation of whose views the use of, and incitement to,
violence plays an essential role. The requirements of freedom, it is
argued, may both ground and set limits to the practice of
toleration.

Toleration and respect for persons

The relationship between toleration and respect for persons is a
concern of the essays by David Edwards and Albert Weale. The
former examines the English Blasphemy Law and its assumptions.
In particular Edwards argues that the most convincing reason for
legally protecting religious convictions against abuse, but not
criticism, is to be found in a principle of respect for persons. Weale
advances a similar view but more generally, and after reviewing
a number of justifications of toleration, concludes that it is the idea

of respect for persons which provides the most convincing case for the virtue of toleration. However, both authors are aware of the tensions which may arise when we aim to be tolerant and show respect for others; the toleration of one set of opinions may, on occasion, appear to involve disregard of, and even disrespect for, the beliefs and sensibilities of others.

Conclusion

These different themes are drawn together by Peter Nicholson in his concluding essay 'Toleration as a moral ideal'. Essentially Nicholson distinguishes two sides to the moral ideal of toleration: the negative and the positive. The negative concerns itself with the reasons there may be against *not* being tolerant. Here the earlier discussions of freedom and harm are pertinent. The positive side of toleration, by contrast, displays toleration as a good in itself – something which is part of treating others as one's equals. Here, the earlier discussions of respect for persons are especially relevant. It is, Nicholson argues, only when these two sides are taken together that the force of toleration as a moral ideal is fully grasped.

Though the practical problems of toleration in contemporary Britain are much less pressing than at the height of the wars of religion or even when Mill feared that a nightmare age of conformism threatened, there are still serious practical and philosophical problems involved in any adequate formulation of a principle of toleration. The contributions in this volume do not address them all, nor do they purport to offer a comprehensive account of toleration. What they do attempt is a serious discussion of some of the most important theoretical problems associated with the practice of toleration in a society such as our own.

Notes

1   J. S. Mill, *On Liberty*. All references are to the Penguin edition, ed. G. Himmelfarb, Harmondsworth, 1974.
2   An interesting introductory historical study on the theory and practice of toleration until the early eighteenth century is H. Kamen, *The Rise of Toleration*, London, 1967.

14

3   J. Milton, *Areopagitica*, reprinted in *John Milton: Selected prose*, ed. C. A. Patrides, Harmondsworth, 1974.

4   B. Spinoza, *Tractatus Theologico-Politicus*, in *The Chief Works of Spinoza*, trans. R. Elwes, New York, 1955, ch. 20.

5   J. Locke, *A Letter on Toleration*, trans. J. W. Gough, Oxford, 1968.

6   op. cit., 68.

7   See for example J. C. Rees, 'A re-reading of Mill on liberty' with a postscript in P. Radcliffe (ed.), *Limits of Liberty: Studies of Mill's On Liberty*, Belmont, 1966; R. Wollheim, 'John Stuart Mill and the limits of state action', *Social Research*, 40, 1973; C. L. Ten, *Mill on Liberty*, Oxford, 1980; J. Gray, *Mill on Liberty: A Defence*, Oxford, 1983.

8   *Report of the Committee on Homosexual Offences and Prostitution*, Cmnd. 247, para. 13, London, 1957.

9   H. L. A. Hart, *Law, Liberty and Morality*, Oxford, 1963; P. Devlin, *The Enforcement of Morals*, Oxford, 1965; H. L. A. Hart, 'Social solidarity and the enforcement of morality', *University of Chicago Law Review*, 35, 1967.

10 P. Devlin, op. cit., 14.

11 op. cit., 119.

12 ibid.

13 ibid.

14 *Obscene Publications Act*, 1959, s.1 (1).

15 *Report of the Committee on Obscenity and Film Censorship*, Cmnd. 7772, part 3, London, 1979.

16 Lord Denning, *Freedom Under the Law*, London, 1949, 46.

17 *R. v. Lemon and Gay News Ltd.*, 1978.

18 ibid.

19 See also Lord Scarman, *Toleration and the Law*, York, 1983.

20 *Race Relations Act*, 1976, s.70.

21 Nigel Fielding, *The National Front*, London, 1981, 174.

1

Toleration, individual differences and respect for persons

ALBERT WEALE

Nothing is more obvious than that people differ from one another. Some are pious, others are irreverent. Some prefer one sexual partner, others prefer a variety. Some are committed to developing their skills and talents to the maximum extent possible, and others are content to allow their lives to pass with passive intoxication of alcohol, television or other sources of gratification. Some seek active involvement in the affairs of the community, others prefer to cultivate their own gardens. And some have very strong views about the way in which their society is to be organized, whilst others are prepared to let everyone go their own way. These differences define the style of life that people adopt. In many respects individuals will share their style of life with other like-minded individuals. Churches and religious groupings are the most obvious example of such sharing. In such groups people will marry, rear children, conduct their economic life or hold opinions that are similar to others who also have the same lifestyle. When individual lifestyles exhibit such socially significant patterns, I shall say that the individuals involved share a distinctive form of life. Like individual lifestyles, forms of life will differ markedly from one another in any complex modern society.

Quite often the fact that different forms of life exist within a community is taken to be a reason for tolerating those forms of life. Individual differences are taken to imply social toleration. The commonly heard saying that one should live and let live expresses this viewpoint, as does the equally common view that individuals should be allowed to do what they like provided they do not harm others. More formally, Robert Nozick offers a similar claim when he proposes that there is not one kind of life that is best for the variety of individuals that exist, and argues that a utopian arrangement would be one in which individuals were free to pursue their own kind of life provided they respected the rights of others.[1]

Clearly there are practical limitations on the extent to which individuals living in the same society can differ from one another in the pattern of life they lead. The need for a common set of laws or customs will restrict the freedom that persons have to pursue their own way of life. However, there may still be scope for considerable divergence within a common set of laws. More importantly, a society may adopt the principle that certain areas of personal conduct should not be restricted at all, so that there are certain matters which, in the famous words of the Wolfenden Report, are 'in brief and crude terms, not the law's business'.[2] A society may go even further than this and say not only that the law should not restrict certain types of conduct, it should also positively protect the ability of an individual to choose his or her conduct in certain matters. The areas of life in which we might expect a special concern for individual differences are those where the meaning of the activity is especially significant for individuals. Sexual practices, the practice of one's religion and the ability to watch, read or listen in private to whatever one wants will be the core of that realm in which individuals should be allowed to pursue their own way of life. Whenever it is said that the ability of persons to choose in these matters should be protected, I shall say that a policy of toleration is being recommended.

The issue I propose to discuss in this essay is what the significance is of individual differences in arguments for social toleration. In what ways, if at all, can we move from noting the fact of variety of individual lifestyle to recommending a public policy of toleration? In discussing this question I shall not be so much concerned with the problem of how we might determine which activities are simply the responsibility of individuals and which have some broader implications. I shall assume that individuals can exhibit some significant differences of personal lifestyle without that restricting their ability to perform the duties of citizenship. That ideas might change on where these boundaries are to be fixed is of less importance than the problem of whether, even granting the existence of a private realm, we have a reason for tolerating diversity. It follows that the issue can be described either as the propriety of keeping the law out of the private realm, or as a restriction on the sort of reasons that can be advanced for favouring some law or public policy rather than others.[3] In either case the ground of the prohibition is supposed to rest on a claim about the importance of individual differences. It is this claim that I am anxious to discuss.

As a final preliminary point I shall just note that two conditions have to be satisfied if the argument from individual difference to social toleration is to have any interest. The first of these conditions is that the individual differences should involve important moral concerns, from at least some points of view. No one is going to argue that it matters for public policy that people have different tastes, that some people for example prefer tea and others coffee. To be tolerant involves the acceptance of differences that really matter to you. If you do not care about people's conduct and preferences, then you are not tolerant in allowing them to do what they want, you are merely indifferent. Indifference and toleration should be clearly distinguished. The second condition to be satisfied is that those who are tolerant could get their way if they chose. If the state tolerates different ways of life, then this implies that it could restrict them if it chose. I shall mark this distinction in terms of the difference between acquiescence and toleration. If the state cannot enforce legislation, as it was impossible to enforce prohibition in the United States, then I shall say that the state acquiesces in a course of action. If it could prevent it, but does not, then I shall say that it tolerates a course of action. Though arguments from the impossibility of enforcement may weigh heavily in day-to-day political decision-making, as they did over prohibition, the most interesting arguments, from the point of view of a political morality, are those where enforcement is possible, but there are reasons for refraining from enforcement. It is to an examination of some of those reasons that I now turn.

Consequentialist reasons

The first reason I shall consider is consequentialist in type. It asserts that the consequences of acting tolerantly are better than the consequences of acting intolerantly. The practice of toleration produces more good on balance than the alternatives.

The consequences of a practice can be usefully divided into those which are direct and those which are indirect. The direct consequences pertain to the effects on those whose behaviour is tolerated under the practice. They comprise such things as the satisfactions that people derive from pursuing their own way of life rather than having an alien way of life imposed upon them. The indirect consequences include the general social benefits that we derive from living in a tolerant society, and include such things as the advantages we derive from living in a society in which there are diverse 'experiments in living', to use Mill's term.[4] Consequential arguments for toleration claim that either the direct or the indirect consequences of toleration, or both, are superior to available alternatives.

In order to illustrate the direct benefits of toleration, consider the example of Alan Turing. Turing was a pioneering researcher into computer languages and artificial intelligence, who during the Second World War led the group that broke the Enigma Code, which the Germans mistakenly considered uncrackable. He was also homosexual, at a time when homosexuality was a legal offence in the United Kingdom. When, after the war, his homosexual activities came to the notice of the Manchester police, he was prosecuted and convicted. For his sentence he was given the choice of a term in prison or hormone treatment. Having chosen the hormone treatment, he spent three years in despair before finally committing suicide in 1954. His premature death, not to mention the anxiety and desperation of his last years, were a direct consequence for Turing of intolerant laws regarding sexual practice. In a more liberal climate he could have lived out his life in a productive and personally satisfying way. The general practice of toleration in sexual matters, it is asserted, will prevent the misery and personal suffering to which people like Turing would otherwise be liable.

The indirect benefits of toleration were stressed by Mill in his

19

defence of liberty and individuality.[5] Mill argued that a number of benefits flow from allowing the free expression of individual character and belief. In the first place, there are those benefits that can be shared by others whether or not they possess their own special degree of individuality. Included in these benefits, we find: that human beings become more noble and beautiful objects of contemplation; that human life becomes richer by diversity, making the race infinitely better worth belonging to; and that an age of individuality is more noteworthy to posterity. In the second place, Mill holds that there are collective benefits to be derived from individual freedom which are especially valuable to those who are not themselves prone to individuality. These benefits may be summarized as example and innovation. Only individuals of strong character will set examples of more enlightened conduct, and unless they are allowed the freedom to set this example the generality of persons will lose the opportunity of witnessing innovative examples with the possible benefits to their own conduct. Innovation, then, is necessary to maintain the progressive character of a society. In the absence of innovation a society will become stationary, and will decline into mere customary ways of life. Mill thought that even a country like China, which had been fortunate in having well-designed customs, could not contribute to the improvement of humankind because its pattern of social life had become merely customary. It stifled the source of innovation, namely individuality. Experiments in living, on this argument, are desirable, not only because they are more directly satisfying to the people who carry them out, but also because they produce diffuse, but none the less genuine, benefits to those who do not participate in them.

There is one further point to be made about the benefits of toleration. Lack of toleration means imposing a way of life upon others. To impose such a way of life involves costs. There has to be a machinery of enforcement which secures the required degree of conformity to a common standard, and which involves diverting resources from productive uses elsewhere. Unless there are positive benefits from intolerance, the existence of costs of enforcement should always mean that toleration is the preferred option, since it is generally cheaper to leave people alone than it is to force them into a particular course of action. In other words, in looking at the argument against toleration we must find, in consequentialist terms, not only benefits that outweigh those of toleration but also benefits that compensate for the costs of enforcement.

Can we find benefits that compensate for the costs of imposing a particular way of life on people, and which outweigh the direct and indirect benefits that are supposed to flow from a policy of toleration? Consider first the direct consequences of toleration. The assumption here is that it is generally more satisfying for people to do what they have chosen to do, rather than act in accordance with somebody else's wishes. The tacit further assumption is that people are better judges of their own welfare than anybody else. No one knows you as you know yourself, and therefore you are in a better position than anyone else to know what is good and what is bad for you. Yet, although this assumption is often made by those defending a policy of toleration, it is rarely substantiated and runs up against some awkward evidence that suggests that as a matter of general principle it may well be false.

It is a clear and obvious fact of liberal democratic political systems that they have a set of institutions that provide extensive welfare provision for all citizens. This welfare provision has a wide variety of purposes, and there is no reason to believe that it serves any overriding objective. However, it is difficult to explain and justify compulsory insurance for health care and retirement benefits unless we invoke the belief that some people would not make adequate provision for themselves, and would therefore be destitute, without their being party to compulsory arrangements.[6] In other words, underlying some of the central institutions of modern liberal democracies there is the belief that persons will not always be the best judges of their own welfare. There is, moreover, no intrinsic limit we can place on those spheres of action in which persons will be good judges of their own welfare and those spheres of action in which they will not be good judges. If people are thought liable to mistake their own interests in terms of their savings behaviour, perhaps they will also mistake their own interests in terms of their sexual behaviour or their choice of literature and films. At most the argument from direct consequences leads to a presumption that individuals should be granted toleration, a presumption that may be overturned by

21

suitable evidence. It does not lead to a generally valid conclusion about the moral desirability of toleration. Moreover, in enforcing conduct that is intended to be in a person's own interests, mistakes will sometimes be made. Turing's treatment at the hands of the authorities was harsh and shameful; but the existence of this sort of example does not show that the enforcement of a general code of sexual practice upon members of society is wrong. Moreover, there are other areas of personal conduct that are less intimately related to one's identity than sexual orientation. Not even the most libertarian defender of pornography asserts that the direct benefit to the reader has some special personal value.

The argument from indirect consequences stressed the general benefits that society derived collectively from allowing experiments in living, provided that they did not harm the interests of others. But this formula begs a number of questions which as John Horton shows ought not to be begged.[7] In particular, there is no uncontroversial definition of harm that can be used in a morally neutral way to adjudicate between competing claims about what is in somebody's interest. The obvious and frequently discussed example of this problem occurs in the issue of whether offence in and of itself constitutes harm. It is integral to Mill's defence of toleration that offence is not a harm, or at least not a harm from which people ought to be protected by society. Yet it is difficult to justify this hard and fast distinction between offence on the one hand and harm on the other. Offence can be felt as keenly as other legally recognized harms such as slander or libel. To rule out offence as a ground of public policy would seem to involve us in taking an unjustifiably restricted or material view about what validly will count as a harm.

The problems both of how individual interests are to be judged and of how harms are to be defined are neatly illustrated in some of the objections to tolerating the sale and consumption of pornography. The objections to the unrestricted sale of pornography are various, but two stand out in particular: individuals degrade themselves through pornography; and they degrade others, particularly women. To consider the latter point first. Women are portrayed in pornography as objects whose use is to gratify others', often violent, sexual desires. In noting this feature of pornography, the claim is that some people can be quite legitimately offended by the knowledge that this portrayal takes place, and that offence of this sort constitutes a harm which merits social protection. Moreover, on the first point, it is objected to pornography that its use is degrading, even when those who consume it do not find it so. In other words those who object to pornography being freely available contest that there is a sphere of self-regarding activity in which the definition of harm to oneself is uncontroversial. As well as participating in a practice whose general effect is to degrade women, those who produce and consume pornography are also degrading themselves.[8] It does not matter for present purposes whether the arguments about pornography are convincing in the particular case. The example does show that the concept of harm is neither self-evident nor uncontroversial. Persons may not be the best judges of their own welfare, and, even if they were, the example they set may not inspire others to emulation and moral innovation, but may merely disgust them, and cause offence.

One conclusion that we can take from the discussion so far is that consequentialist considerations do not provide generally valid grounds for a policy of toleration. Neither direct nor indirect consequences provide reasons for generally favouring a policy of toleration, although they may on occasion be effective in that respect. Another conclusion that we can draw concerns the reason for this failure. Consequences have to be evaluated, and their value will be judged inconsistently by those adopting different moral points of view. This difference of judgement would appear to represent a radical defect at the heart of consequentialist reasoning. In order to overcome this defect, it would seem necessary to go beyond these competing points of view. The next set of arguments we shall consider aims to do precisely this, by establishing principles of toleration in terms of an impartial moral outlook. This is the contractarian argument.

Contractarian reasons

The outline of contractarian arguments is simple enough, although in their detailed development they tend to become somewhat complicated.[9] Principles regulating social life are fair if they would be agreed upon by persons ignorant of their own particular circumstances but negotiating with others over the definition of common principles to govern the terms of their association. For example, in a contractarian approach to the issue of pornography we are to imagine that persons have to agree on a set of principles for dealing with pornography without knowing whether they are themselves male or female. The claim of contractarian theorists is that the results of this hypothetical reasoning define fair principles of social choice. By asking people to define principles outside a specific point of view, the hope is that they can impartially agree a common set of principles.

A specific version of this argument is proposed by Rawls when discussing the principle of religious toleration.[10] According to this argument those people who are involved in the contractual bargain know which society they belong to, but they do not know their own personal characteristics. In particular, people have to reckon with the possibility that they may turn out in practice to have any of the religious beliefs that are currently prevalent in their society. Ignorant of their own religious views, contracting parties face the prospect of having to legislate for the framework of religious practice, without knowing which religion, if any, they favour. Rawls argues that contracting parties who were ignorant in this way would nevertheless recognize that believers of all sorts of religions attach great importance to the freedom to practise their religion and worship in the way that they please. With this recognition in mind they would converge on the view that a fair framework for diverse religious practices would be one in which all persons had the equal right to freedom of religious conscience and practice. In other words, the existence of diverse religious convictions and practice would lead to a principle of mutual toleration, in a situation in which persons were forced to legislate in an impartial way.

Does this Rawlsian argument provide a solution for how arguments for toleration in general might be framed? There are considerable difficulties in thinking that it does. The conclusion that Rawls believes he has established is that the practice of sincere minority belief is protected from control by numerically superior adherents of alternative creeds. The confessional state is to be rejected. But the argument that Rawls advances could be used to establish also a quite different conclusion, namely that a minority

24

of religious persons could fairly be given the right to impose a particular form of life upon the non-religious. For example, suppose a fundamentalist religious group feels strongly that business should not be conducted on the Sabbath. Ignorant of their future positions, contracting parties might think that this was an issue on which the religious felt intensely, whereas the non-religious were concerned in only a marginal way. In such a situation, potential offensiveness to religious sentiments might be regarded as a valid ground for legislation. The non-religious might not, therefore, enjoy with the religious the equal right to act in accordance with their convictions on the Sabbath. More generally, Rawls's decision procedure will yield a principle of toleration when the contracting parties are contemplating the diverse convictions of those who hold strong religious beliefs, but it will not yield the principle of toleration when intensity of feeling among the religious is matched with lack of intensity of the non-religious. The equal right of all persons to act in accordance with their convictions is not an implication of the contractarian argument.

Another difficulty for the contractarian position is that it is not clear how it can provide a model for deciding on other, controversial issues of toleration. Revert to the example of pornography. It is difficult to see how a contractarian procedure could settle the rival claims of those who assert that pornography is degrading, both to consumers and to women in general, and those who assert that people should be free to produce and consume pornography as they choose. When we consider competing religious beliefs, we have some reason for thinking that the depth of conviction is likely to be balanced on both sides. When we turn, by contrast, to the rival assertions of those in the pornography debate, there is no obvious way by which we can assess depth of feeling on either side. Moreover, the contractarian procedure does not seem to capture the exact moral disagreement that is involved in the pornography dispute. The parties to that dispute do not simply disagree about the strength of feelings involved; they also disagree about the moral character that those feelings have. This disagreement is not captured in the contractarian procedure.

For these reasons I conclude that one cannot build an adequate principle of toleration upon contractarian foundations.

The principle of neutrality

If neither consequentialist nor contractarian arguments provide general reasons for favouring toleration, perhaps we can turn to a principle that is sometimes directly invoked in defence of liberal legislation? The principle I have in mind is the principle of neutrality. This requires that the state and the public authorities be above a commitment to any particular form of life.[11] The standard case illustrating the practice of the principle is the absence of an established church in the United States. By prohibiting the establishment of any religion, it is argued that the state is kept neutral between competing claims. A policy of neutrality would guarantee that legislation concerned with personal behaviour would not endorse one way of life against any other. For example, monogamy would not be given special status compared to polygamy or polyandry. Neutrality, in this sense, is not seen as the principle that would emerge from a hypothetical fair bargaining game. Nor is it seen as a policy that would promote the best consequences judged in terms of the satisfaction of desires or the promotion of social progress. It is instead seen as an ideal in its own right. It is, moreover, an ideal that might be thought to have a natural affinity with a liberal principle of toleration, since it requires states to refrain from endorsing a particular way of life. It would therefore seem to provide a bridge between the existence of individual differences and a social policy of toleration.

It is sometimes suggested that there are obvious practical ob-jections to a state pursuing a policy of neutrality. For example, any society would appear to need for its survival a set of common cultural standards. These common standards will define ways of life for those who are educated into them, thus implicitly re-stricting the range of options that are available to people as they grow up. For example, being taught any particular natural language will condition one's thought and habits of feeling. Although this objection to the principle of neutrality has some force, it typically underestimates the ingenuity that societies can show in coping with cultural diversity. A multi-lingual and multi-ethnic society like Yugoslavia may exhibit considerable frictions between its constituent units, but those frictions will not necessarily threaten the existence of the society itself. In any case,

26

the idea of neutrality, like any other ideal, needs only to be pursued as far as is practically feasible. That, in any one case, it cannot be taken to its logical limits is not an argument against the validity of the ideal itself.

The fundamental problem in using the idea of neutrality as the underlying value of toleration is that it is extremely difficult to specify the content of the ideal. There are at least two questions which need to be answered before content can be given to the idea of neutrality. Is neutrality an intentional or a causal concept? And does it involve mere absence of intervention or does it require positive action?[12]

Consider, for example, the problem of whether neutrality is an intentional concept or a causal one. It may be that by its policies the state does not intend to favour certain ways of life rather than others, but the effect of certain policies may well be to advantage certain ways of life at the expense of others. For example, if all restrictions on hours and times of trading for shops were abolished, the effect of this change might well be to make it more difficult for those who seek to follow a traditional religious way of life to continue to trade in a commercially profitable way. The growth of Sunday trading makes it more difficult for Christian shop-keepers to compete in the market, and therefore makes it more difficult for them to maintain their economic activities as well as their religious commitment. If neutrality is thought of as an intentional concept, then this consequence of the change need not be thought of as a breach of neutrality. No one has intended that Christian shopkeepers be disadvantaged by the change; it merely works out that they are. On the other hand, if neutrality is taken to be a causal concept then the change will amount to a breach of neutrality. The effect of the change is to create a disadvantage that was not there in the first place. The effect of the legislative change is to impose an extra burden upon Christian traders compared to their secular competitors.

A further respect in which the principle of neutrality needs to be specified is in terms of the contrast between absence of intervention and positive support. It may well be that in the absence of positive support from the state certain minority ways of life will be eroded. This is often true in the case of minority language groups. By doing nothing to promote bilingualism, the state may allow the demise of a minority language, so that for example the Welsh language, in the absence of positive policies, would go the way of Cornish. To prevent this happening the state will have to undertake positive policies ranging from provision of teaching resources through to support for the media, in, say, the form of a special television channel. Here again the implications of neutrality are unclear and indeterminate. If we adopt one interpretation of the neutrality principle, then one course of action will follow. If we adopt another interpretation then a contrary course of action will follow. Neither interpretation is self-evident.

In order to choose between these divergent interpretations, we should need to understand in more detail the ethical basis of the neutrality principle. In order to obtain an idea of this basis, consider what might seem to be a paradoxical feature of the neutrality principle itself. When applied to policies and practices governing incompatible ways of life, it presupposes ethical diversity; and yet its application presupposes ethical agreement that it is the correct principle to apply. Is it really consistent to have this mixture of great diversity and ethical convergence? Why should people who may disagree fundamentally on how to live their lives, nevertheless come to agree on how the public regulation of their conduct should be organized? The answer, I suggest, is that behind the principle of neutrality there lies the value of equal respect for persons. It is this value which needs to be examined if we are to understand properly how there can be an argument from individual differences to social toleration.

Respect for persons

The concept of respect for persons is of itself somewhat vague. But for present purposes I shall take it to comprise three ideas. The first is that persons have goals and purposes in their lives that are meaningful for them. The second is that persons are capable of reflecting upon their circumstances and act on reasons that derive from these reflections. The third is that the goals that give meaning to people's lives are the product of their reflection, so that their goals are in part self-chosen, and derive a portion of their value from that fact. Respect for persons therefore involves the claim that persons should be allowed to act on their own conception of what is good and valuable for them, and that in so far as they are doing this they are expressing their natures as rational and reflective beings.

Understood in this way the value of respect immediately implies a presumption in favour of toleration, since a tolerant society is one which allows persons the freedom to act on their own self-chosen values. However, although establishing a presumption in favour of toleration, the concept of respect, taken in itself, does not rule out the sort of paternalism which, as we saw in the case of consequentialist arguments, might provide reasons for limiting a person's freedom of action. One can respect another as the author of his or her own values, without tolerating all the choices that the person makes. A concern for the well-being of persons might lead to paternalistic restrictions on their freedom of action, which might not be strictly inconsistent with the value of respect. To provide a general argument for toleration we need a concept of *equal* respect. That is, persons have to respect one another as equals, this respect implying that each person recognizes others as capable and competent to form their own projects and plans of life.

When equality of respect is taken seriously as a value, it will limit the possibility of a government devising and implementing paternalistic legislation. It is inconsistent with equality of respect for one group of people to impose restrictions on another group for the purpose of protecting the 'weaker brethren' from themselves. Limitations on sexual behaviour, or restrictions on freedom of speech or association, would not be justified in so far as they were designed to protect people from the consequences of their own misguided choices. The principle of equal respect does not imply that persons are generally the best judges of their own welfare; but it still does not license paternalism in those cases where one group of people judge, perhaps rightly from their point of view, that others are deficient judges. Equal respect implies that people's judgements have value because they are the expressions of how people have chosen to lead their own lives.

Does this mean that no paternalistic legislation is ever justified? Not necessarily. On some occasions paternalistic laws and regulations will be justified not on the grounds that some persons are incompetent to make decisions, but on the grounds that all of us, even the most competent, are sometimes in situations where our judgements are misguided. Much health and safety legislation can be justified on these grounds. It is difficult for even competent individuals to know whether products and practices are safe, and so we impose restrictions or requirements on ourselves, for example safety precautions in factories, in order to make sure that our everyday decisions are sensible. This sort of legislation we may call 'democratic' paternalism. It does not rest on the assumption that some people or practices are intrinsically superior to others; it requires merely that we all recognize there are occasions when any of us is prone to lapses. Democratic paternalism does not violate the principle of equal respect in a way that other variants of paternalism do.

The principle of equal respect also enables us to understand what is wrong with the contractarian approach to the problem of toleration. The difficulty we noted in that approach lay in the possibility that the intense preferences of a minority of persons could legislate for a majority. If the minority feels strongly enough about the manner in which the majority should behave, then there is nothing in the contractarian approach to prevent the minority's wishes becoming the social choice. Clearly, however, the imposition by one group of people of preferences about how others are to conduct their personal lives violates the principle of equal respect. It is not consistent with an equal respect for persons to legislate for them to adopt your self-chosen values rather than their own self-chosen values.

The principle of equal respect provides us with a reason for rejecting consequentialist and contractarian arguments where they suggest that society should be intolerant of differences among individuals. Does the principle help us to reduce the ambiguities of the neutrality principle? Equal respect may only require that we remove any obstacles in the way of people pursuing their own way of life, intentionally leaving them free to do whatever they wish. Equal respect, in this case, means that neutrality would be an intentional and negative concept. Equal respect for people's sexual practices probably only requires neutrality in this sense. The abolition of laws forbidding certain types of sexual acts between consenting adults in private is likely to be sufficient to secure a regime of neutrality with respect to sexual matters. However,

there are some spheres of social activity in which the principle of
equal respect would imply that neutrality was a positive as well
as an intentional concept. To see why let us first examine why
neutrality must be intentional, and may be positive, if the principle
of equal respect is to be pursued.

Consider the case of someone who does not wish to work on
a day which he or she regards as holy, but who lives in a generally
secular society.[13] According to the principle of equal respect such
a person has no valid claim to the effect that the state should enforce
his or her particular day as a day of rest for the society at large,
since this would impose upon the secular majority a way of life
that they had not chosen themselves. This conclusion would stand
even if the general effect of liberal legislation were to undermine
the religious way of life. The reason is that if we adopt a causal
interpretation of the principle of neutrality, then we cannot be
neutral between different forms of life requiring incompatible
social environments for their maintenance. If we judge the state's
actions in terms of its effects, then it cannot show equal respect for
incompatible ways of life. If we judge the state's actions in terms
of intentions, however, then the intention of the legislation is to
permit persons to treat certain days as holy if they so choose, but
not to force them into this recognition if they do not so choose.

However, this does not mean that the state is forbidden to take
special steps to protect the minority. Because it does not enforce
general observance of the particular group's practices, it is still
possible for the state to give positive help to members of the group
to protect their way of life in a harsh environment. For example,
the state might require employers to adapt their working routines,
where this is feasible, to protect the practices of a minority, or it
might grant tax-exemption to the schools and other educational
institutions of a minority. These measures will impose some
economic costs upon the general population, but they will not
limit the freedom of the general population to do with their lives
what they will. Equal respect is being maintained because no one
is being forced into practices that are alien to them, and yet some
measure of positive protection is being afforded to those whose
way of life is threatened by the general practice of toleration. It
may well be that these positive measures fall short of what is
required to ensure that particular minority ways of life are

31

preserved. It may be that some ways of life do require general conformity within society for them to be maintained. But as it would breach the principle of equal respect to impose general conformity we do not hold that a neutral state must be successful in protecting all forms of life. We do hold that it should not set out deliberately to destroy forms of life, and should give some positive help to those who are disadvantaged by a general practice.

How does the principle of equal respect fare when applied to the case of pornography? The regulation of pornographic material in English law is traditionally based on the test of whether such material has 'a tendency to deprave and corrupt'. As Susan Mendus shows in her paper, this test becomes hopelessly confused in practice, partly because the notion of 'tendency' is ambiguous and partly because of the difficulties of producing sufficient evidence that on any one occasion a particular piece of pornography does tend to deprave and corrupt.[14] However, there is another objection to the obscenity law apart from the practical difficulties it encounters. This is that it rests upon a paternalistic premiss, involving the judgement that those who resort to pornographic material have adopted a moral scheme that is less worthy of respect than others and that their freely chosen activity should therefore be restricted. The principle of equal respect would seem to imply that there should be no laws restricting the production and sale of pornography, and that a community founded on the principle of respect would allow all its members equal access to whatever literature and so on they wished to buy.

However, before jumping to this conclusion, we should pause to note one objection to pornography which does not incur the difficulties of the 'deprave and corrupt' test. This is the claim that pornography, in and of itself, represents women, as Susan Mendus put it, 'as objects and inferiors'.[15] This claim amounts to the assertion that a willingness to allow the existence of pornographic material fails to treat women as entitled to equal respect. Instead it fosters a society in which their status is affirmed to be inferior, rather as the representation of blacks as servants and farmhands in much American entertainment fostered the belief in the inferiority of the descendants of plantation slaves. A concern with the principle of equal respect might lead us to wish to prohibit the product and sale of certain types of material, in order to affirm the

32

status of women as equal members of the political community.

Putting these two points together it appears that the principle of equal respect implies contradictory prescriptions. On the one hand, when applied to those who wish to be exposed to pornographic material, it suggests a policy of toleration. On the other hand, when we consider how a policy of toleration creates a climate of opinion in which women are deemed inferior, it suggests a policy of restriction. We have an instance here of something that is familiar in both morals and politics, namely a clash of rights between two sets of people. There does not appear to be any theoretical way of adjudicating between these rival claims. Instead it is a matter of judgement, in individual cases, how far the rival claims are supported by the principle of equal respect. From our point of view the most interesting aspect is that the conflict over pornography can be seen as a clash of rights arising from an application of the principle of equal respect, and the notions of depravity and corruption do not need to be introduced.

So far I have argued that the principle of equal respect does what none of the competing principles are able to do, namely provide a bridge between the acknowledgement of individual differences and the proposal to practise social toleration. However, the principle of equal respect is a strong one, and it too may be thought to require some justification, or at least supporting argument. I have only the space here to sketch an argument that I have developed at length elsewhere,[16] but I hope that this sketch serves to provide some motive for thinking that a principle of equal respect might provide a plausible basis for toleration.

Let us consider two ways in which the principle of equal respect might be violated. The first is a simple and cynical manipulation of the power of the state for one's own purposes. In this mode the person who breaches the principle of equal respect acknowledges that persons are capable of formulating their own plans and projects, but chooses to ignore this inconvenient recognition because it prevents the attainment of some particular political purpose. I take it to be intrinsic to such situations that such manipulators cannot offer a reason of principle for having their own way. They are not using the power of the state for any justifiable purpose. They deserve whatever is coming to them (alas, it all too often arrives late). The second situation does involve an argument of principle, however, for this involves the person who honestly believes that some persons and their choices should be less respected than others. There are some conscientious and thoughtful people who adopt this position. They are, however, in a dilemma, since the position they adopt makes it difficult, if not impossible, for them to justify their position to the people who would be adversely affected by its implementation. To be able to explain to these people why their personal choices were given less weight than the choices of others presupposes that those being addressed have the capacity to understand and act upon the arguments advanced. But if they are capable of this degree of reflective capacity, how does it arise that they are incapable of making personal choices? The logic of those political positions that deny the principle of equal respect is to drive towards extravagant and wildly implausible claims about the innate inferiority of certain types of human being. This is a high price to pay for violating the principle of equal respect.

The principle of equal respect finds its grounds therefore in the dilemma that the use of political power has to be justified. In offering such a justification we presuppose that members of a political community can act on the reasons that are advanced. The same motive that leads to restrictions on tyranny also leads in the direction of social toleration.

Notes

1 R. Nozick, *Anarchy, State and Utopia*, Oxford, 1974, 310.
2 *Report of the Committee on Homosexual Offences and Prostitution*, Cmnd. 247, para. 24, London, 1957.
3 This is intended to accommodate the claims of C. L. Ten, *Mill on Liberty*, Oxford, 1980, 40.
4 J. S. Mill, *On Liberty*, in *Utilitarianism, Liberty and Considerations on Representative Government*, ed. H. B. Acton, London, 1972, 115.
5 ibid., 114–31.
6 For a discussion on this argument see the essay by Peter Jones in this volume.
7 See the essay by John Horton in this volume.
8 See the essay by Susan Mendus in this volume.

9   The most well-known exposition of contract theory is to be found in J. Rawls, *A Theory of Justice*, Oxford, 1972.

10 ibid., 205–16.

11 For political theories resting on this principle see B. A. Ackerman, *Social Justice in the Liberal State*, New Haven, 1980, and R. Dworkin, *Taking Rights Seriously*, London, 1978.

12 Compare A. Montefiore (ed.), *Neutrality and Impartiality*, Cambridge, 1975, 3–45, and J. Raz, 'Liberalism, autonomy and the politics of neutral concern', in *Midwest Studies in Philosophy*, 7, 1982.

13 This example, taken from a case brought at English law, is discussed by Lord Scarman in his J. B. and W. B. Morrell Memorial Lecture of 1983, *Toleration and the Law*, York.

14 See the essay by Susan Mendus in this volume.

15 ibid.

16 See Albert Weale, *Political Theory and Social Policy*, London, 1983, ch. 3.

2

Toleration and the right to freedom

THOMAS BALDWIN

There are many circumstances in which it is prudent for states to be tolerant towards their citizens. In some circumstances, however, toleration is thought to be not just a matter of prudence, but of duty. This duty is plausibly interpreted as arising from a right, possessed by citizens, to be tolerated. Such a right has often been held to be a right to freedom. My initial aim in this essay is to examine our right to freedom, by examining both the freedom to which we can plausibly claim to have a right and the grounds for supposing that we do have a right to this freedom. It will emerge that the duty to tolerate does not only arise from a right to freedom. There is another more explicitly political right which lies at the basis of the duty to tolerate.

★

I shall commence my examination of our right to freedom with Locke's political theory. It is appropriate to begin in this way because of Locke's famous defence of religious toleration, but I shall concentrate on Locke's *Two Treatises of Government*[1] in which he propounds the political theory which underlies the argument of his defence of religious toleration (the application of the theory to religious toleration is already suggested in the Second *Treatise*).[2] Although Locke's theory has many shortcomings, some of which I shall discuss, it is, I think, only by appropriating for ourselves his insights that we can find our way to the truth about these matters.

36

Locke begins his *Two Treatises* by affirming that all men have a right to 'natural freedom'.[3] This natural freedom is not a 'licence' to do just as one pleases; instead it is a freedom conditioned by morality, or, as Locke puts it, by 'natural law'.[4] Locke thinks of the strict morality of duty and obligation as a system of laws which manifest our nature as rational beings who have been created by a benevolent God (we shall return to this conception of morality later). Thus since our right to natural freedom gives us no right to act contrary to natural law, it gives us no right to act in breach of duty or obligation, a point of central importance not only to Locke's theory, but to any acceptable theory of freedom. To examine Locke's theory further, we need to look more closely at his conception of natural freedom, at its subjects (*who* is free), the constraints upon it (what one who is free is free *from*), and the ends appropriate to it (what one who is free is free *to*). First, the subjects: these, Locke makes clear, are not human beings as such, but rational beings – 'we are born free, as we are born Rational'.[5] The explanation for this reference to rationality concerns the dependence of natural freedom upon the morality of natural law and is filled out in two ways: the first, simpler, way is that Locke takes rationality to be both necessary and sufficient for knowledge of natural law; hence rational beings are alone in a position to conduct themselves in accordance with the morality of natural law and thus be free. The second way is implied in a passage where Locke writes that reason is the law of nature (and not just that reason instructs us in this law).[6] This suggests the traditional view that natural law is inherently rational, and thus that only those who live by it, as opposed to knowing it, are rational.[7] The constraint especially relevant to natural freedom is political authority. Natural freedom is freedom from all political authority, and Locke's central claim in his dispute with Sir Robert Filmer was that since all rational beings have a right to this freedom, political authority is only legitimate where citizens waive this right by consenting to authority.[8] However, natural freedom is not just freedom from political authority; it also requires that other people should not so interfere with one as to prevent one from enjoying the ends of the freedom – roughly, doing as one chooses, within the limits of the morality of natural law, with what is one's own. It is because of the possibility of constraints of this kind on natural

37

freedom that there is no guarantee of natural freedom within a pre-political state of nature: the state of nature becomes a state of war just where people lose their natural freedom, though not their right to it, whilst remaining not subject to any political authority. Furthermore, to look ahead a bit, it is because of this way of losing one's natural freedom that Locke can say that political authority is instituted to preserve freedom,[9] though this remark is *prima facie* paradoxical since the freedom thus preserved cannot be one's full natural freedom. Concerning the ends of natural freedom it is not now necessary to say much, except to stress that they exclude acts or states which are not morally permissible. Locke puts it thus: a man's freedom is his 'liberty to dispose, and order, as he lists, his Person, Actions, Possessions, and his whole Property, within the Allowance of those Laws under which he is; and therein not to be subject to the arbitrary Will of another, but freely follow his own'.[10]

As we have seen, Locke holds that there is an intrinsic connection between the morality of natural law and our natural freedom. Since he holds that this natural freedom is the basis of all freedoms, he takes it that this connection embodies a general truth about freedom as such. What is supposed to found this connection is a conception of man that is both theological and rationalist. On the one hand, natural law is God's will, and since we are God's creatures, it is the law in accordance with which we have been created. On the other hand, natural law is reason, and, therefore, as rational beings, we are committed to its observance. Hence, either way natural law expresses the fundamental principles of our being, so that if we take it that to be free is to act in accordance with our own nature, as divine or rational creatures, it will follow that the morality of natural law does not constrain, but 'preserves and enlarges' our freedom.[11] So much follows *if* we take it that to be free is to act in accordance with our own nature. And to view Locke in this way is, familiarly enough, to find 'positive' elements within his conception of freedom.[12] It is not easy to give a brief answer to the question as to whether this interpretation of Locke is justified, but we do not need to do so here. For, reverting to Locke's opening doctrine that we have a right to natural freedom, we can take his view to be that natural freedom is the only freedom to which we have a natural right. Given this way of looking at the issue, it would not be necessary to deny that licence is a freedom of sorts (even Locke calls it a 'Liberty');[13] all one needs to say is that there is no natural right to this freedom. Furthermore, the role of natural law in the definition of natural freedom now becomes relatively unproblematic: it is much easier to see how the only freedom to which we have a natural right is freedom conditioned by the strict morality of natural law than it is to see that such a freedom is the only real freedom. The result, therefore, is that one can drop the 'positive' elements from Locke's conception of freedom if one switches from the question of 'What, really, is freedom?' to the question. 'To what freedom do we have a natural right?' Admittedly, the considerations that Locke advances to support his claim that natural freedom is the only genuine freedom – considerations having to do with our nature as rational or divine beings – still have a role as justifications for supposing that we have natural rights at all. But since they have to occur there anyway, it is conceptually clearer to remove them from the generic account of freedom as such.

A different complexity in Locke's account of natural freedom arises from the fact that a right to freedom occurs within natural law itself.[14] For this seems to set up an unhappy circularity: natural freedom is defined in terms of natural law which itself includes a right to freedom. This prompts the question as to which comes first – freedom or natural law? Locke's reply will be that they both come together; but it is, none the less, worth spelling out how it is that a right to freedom can occur within natural law without harmful circularity in the definition of natural freedom. I think this is best achieved through a step-by-step account of natural law. Define *basic* natural law as the duty of respect for the rights of life, health, limbs, and possessions of others; then, as far as this basic natural law goes, we are free to do as we choose as long as these basic natural rights of others are respected. This freedom, however, is only an absence of duty to act otherwise on our part, and nothing so far requires that others are under any duty to respect it. So, to get from *basic* natural law to *full* natural law, we have to add that this freedom is itself to be treated as a right. However, and this is the ground for the apparent circularity described above, once this freedom becomes a right, it must recur within its own specification. For if everyone has a right to this freedom, then it must occur as a limitation on the admissible ends of the freedom itself. The freedom to which we are to have a right cannot be just the freedom to do what we like within basic natural law; for once this freedom is a right of all, each person's freedom is further limited by everyone else's right to freedom, i.e. it is limited to actions which fall within full natural law.

In this way the interdependence of freedom and natural law can be elucidated without circularity. There are, however, two points worth stressing here. First, it is crucial that there be some content to the strict morality of natural law other than respect for a right to freedom. For without a 'basic' natural law by reference to which a freedom can be defined without reference to the right to freedom itself, the circularity involved in the specification of a right to a freedom conditioned by natural law is vicious. Secondly, in one respect the account I have given is misleading in so far as it seems to suggest that the freedom to which we have a right must always be 'recessive', in the sense that it must always give way to other 'dominant' rights. Thus if these other rights are extensive, it seems that the freedom to which we have a right must be correspond- ingly restricted. In one way this is indeed correct. For example, if there is a right not to be offended by others, then the freedom of action to which we have a right must be correspondingly re- stricted. But one can use this very implication to argue against such an extensive right to the absence of offence. That is, the fact that the freedom to which we have a right must be conditioned by rights other than the right to freedom does not show that it lacks intrinsic importance for us, and that we cannot insist on this importance in repudiating the ascription of a right which would dramatically curtail it. As a matter of definition, the freedom to which we have a right has to be specified after other rights: but this order need not match the order of the significance to us of these rights.

It seems at first clear that the freedom thus defined, that to which the full natural law assigns us as a right, is Locke's natural freedom. Yet the manner in which I approached it admits of a certain vagueness here; for I defined it primarily by reference to its ends, as freedom to act as one chooses within natural law, and the constraints were left unspecified. In particular, therefore, it is unspecified whether all political authority is a constraint on this freedom. It seems to me that Locke exploits this unspecificity. For, as I mentioned, since he explicitly regards political society as instituted to preserve freedom he must be operating with a conception of freedom which is not necessarily constrained by political authority, and which is, therefore, not natural freedom. Yet since this freedom must be a freedom to which we have a right (otherwise we could not justly seek to preserve it), it seems now that it competes with our right to natural freedom. The way to resolve this issue is to take it that the fundamental freedom to which we have a right is that which I defined just now – a right to act as one chooses provided that one respects the rights of others in doing so. Such a freedom is basically a freedom from interference by other agents. I shall call this freedom our 'rightful' freedom; we can now ask whether political authority of all kinds is a constraint on our rightful freedom. The answer to this, I think, lies in the further question as to what institutions are intrinsic to the possession of and respect for rights. For it seems clear that whatever institutions are thus intrinsic cannot be a constraint on our rightful freedom, since this freedom is defined in terms of respect for other possessors of rights. Locke suggests, plausibly, that there are three institutions intrinsic to the possession of, and respect for, rights: institutions which define rights ('legislative'), settle disputes ('judicial'), and enforce sanctions on those who violate rights ('executive'). The proper operation of these institutions, therefore, is not a constraint on rightful freedom. But, how, in a given situation are these institutions to be realized? Locke, I think, makes an unargued anarchist assumption that they are fundamentally realized in the absence of all political authority, with each of us legislator, judge, and executive for all others. It seems to me that there is no reason for this assumption. Whatever the merits of anarchism, the point here concerns the realization of the institutions intrinsic to respect for any possession of rights; and the anarchist cannot claim intrinsic superiority for an anarchist realization of them, rather than an explicitly political one. The most one can say is that it is only those institutions which, while effective for their proper ends, involve minimal interference with subjects that are not a constraint on rightful freedom. Thus under conditions (if any) in which anarchist institutions can be effective, all political authority will be constraint on rightful freedom because involving more than minimal interference. But nothing follows from this about conditions under which anarchist institutions are ineffective (which I take to include all conditions to be realistically envisaged for human life); if, under these conditions, effective, though minimal, institutions require political authority, then the exercise of that authority will not be a constraint on rightful freedom.

The outcome, therefore, is that the basic freedom to which we have a right is our rightful freedom and it is this freedom of which Locke writes when he writes of political society as instituted to preserve freedom. The puzzle is that he also writes of our right to natural freedom, freedom from all political authority. The solution to this puzzle is that, under the conditions in which anarchism is possible (roughly the Garden of Eden), our rightful freedom is natural freedom. But what does not follow is that, under different conditions (after the Fall), our rightful freedom is still natural freedom. Locke shows that he recognizes this point when he writes that political society preserves freedom. But he cannot bring this admission to the surface of his argument because it would undermine his case against Filmer, to the effect that all legitimate political authority requires consent. However, since we lack that practical interest in refuting Filmer, the thought that our rightful freedom is natural freedom must appear less attractive to us. The interesting issue that then arises, if our rightful freedom does not exclude political authority, is what connection there is between our rightful freedom and our political rights, respect for which imposes duties of toleration on others.

★

Locke's claim that we have a right to freedom is inseparable from his commitment to natural law. The latter, as we have seen, admits of both a theological and rationalist interpretation. We must now, perhaps regretfully, dispense with the theology: and despite his analogy between geometry and ethics, Locke notoriously fails to deliver a quasi-Euclidean account of natural law.[15] The question that therefore arises is whether one can hope to provide a rational justification for a right to freedom, and, further, whether the right thus justified is a right to natural freedom. These are, of course,

42

among the central issues of eighteenth-century political theory, and of much subsequent political theory. None the less, I think that Locke's account of natural law is a good place from which to start because it does not pretend to provide an account of the whole of virtue; the strict morality of natural law does not comprehend the ideal morality of personal excellence. Our values are not all of one kind, and it is futile to attempt a rationalist foundation for all of them.[16] If pure practical reason is somehow to yield a foundation for values, this can only be so for some values – those which aspire to be, in some sense, universal. Locke's natural law embodies this aspiration for universality; and this makes it an obvious candidate for a rationalist theory, though there is room for scepticism about some aspects of Locke's natural law, especially his treatment of property, which I do not propose to discuss here.

I shall concentrate on the right to freedom, but as I stressed before, if our right to freedom is to have a coherent content, it must be a freedom defined initially in terms of other rights ('basic' natural law). So the question of a rational foundation for the right to freedom can only arise within the context of a rational foundation for other 'basic' rights. Since the content of these rights is, in part, specified by contingent needs and desires, if anything is to have an exclusively rational foundation, it can only be a more abstract principle of right. Thus we arrive at the thought that the theory of rights rests on a single abstract principle of right – the right that each person's fundamental interests be respected. Is this right distinctively rational? Much here depends upon what rationality amounts to. According to one tradition rationality is necessity: in this case, the necessity of the fundamental right of respect, or that of the correlated duty, is supposed to be inherent in the use of moral concepts.[17] But this supposition is implausible unless it is rendered trivially analytic by a question-begging definition of morality. For the only relevant strictly logical feature of moral concepts is that there can only be a moral distinction between situations between which there is also a non-moral distinction. But this is far too weak to yield any categorical claims of right;[18] yet perhaps some weaker claims are defensible. One route here is to interpret 'rational' as 'self-interested'. This may seem to lead to no more than a Hobbesian theory of prudential rationality, which falls short of the intended goal, since it allows for situations in which respect for others clashes with self-interest. But perhaps this outcome can be avoided by a more thorough account of the interests of self.

If we separate interests from present desires (as we must, anyway), and regard the self as somehow intrinsically social, can we not derive an intrinsic connection between self-interest and respect for others? It would be satisfying if this could be demonstrated. A good opening move is to introduce Hegel's Master/ Slave argument, which does indeed seem to show that self-consciousness, and thus self-interest, requires respect for others, as subjects of consciousness whose confirming consciousness of oneself validates one's immediate self-consciousness because it is consciousness of subjects whom one respects oneself.[19] The idea is that we can only achieve self-respect through finding ourselves respected by others whom we ourselves respect. The trouble with this argument is that it only yields a ground for respect for some others, not all of them (as Sartre once forcefully observed).[20] It seems to me that the only way to get beyond this unsatisfactory result, while limiting oneself to self-interest as a premiss, is to moralize the self thoroughly: to claim that we are inherently moral beings, intrinsically committed to respect for others. Green provides a lucid formulation of this thought:

> Now the self of which a man thus forecasts the fulfilment, is not an abstract or empty self. It is a self already affected in the most primitive forms of human life by manifold interests, among which are interests in other persons. These are not merely interests dependent on other persons for the means to their gratification, but interests in the good of those other persons, interests which cannot be satisfied without the consciousness that those other persons are satisfied.[21]

This produces the right result; but it seems to beg the question – or at least just to shift the question from one as to the justification for taking the right of respect as rational to one as to the justification for supposing the self to be thus inherently committed to respect for all others. The Hegelian argument provides some ground for this view, but, not yet enough. Furthermore, views which thus moralize the self tend to pay too little attention to the

44

separate identity of different selves; if we are, fundamentally, just aspects of a single self-realizing principle of perfection (as Green held), then doubtless respect for all others is intrinsic to each of us. But, as Sidgwick icily observed, no such account can do justice to the situation of one who finds himself required to sacrifice himself on behalf of others.[22] In the end, indeed, accounts of this kind appear to be more or less secular variants of the natural theology Locke espoused. Once natural theology is regarded as untenable, so, too, are accounts which in this way moralize the self.

Is there any other way to justify the rationality of a fundamental right of respect? I want to explore one candidate. It has frequently been observed that although egoism is not inherently incoherent, it is a motive that dare not speak its name. That is, the egoist cannot present his egoism to others as a reason for them to act in ways favourable to him. If he is to offer another a reason for action, the reason must somehow appeal to the other's concerns in such a way that the other is motivated to act; and it clearly cannot do so if it requires that the other's fundamental interests be disregarded (assuming that the other knows what these are). In this sense, therefore, proffered reasons for action, whether proffered with a view to ultimate self-interest or not, must manifest respect for their audience. It does not follow that they must manifest respect for everyone; even if thieves speak of honour among themselves, they need not do so of their victims. But what does follow is that reasons for action which are intended to appeal to just anyone must manifest respect for all; and in this sense one can then claim for the right of respect that it has a certain 'dialectical rationality', in that it cannot be violated without pragmatic incoherence in proposals that are to provide reasons for action for just anyone. What might such proposals be? Well, political proposals seem to provide an example, and perhaps the only example of any practical interest. Their universality derives not from the thought that they ought to make an appeal to everyone – that would beg the question; but, rather, that if they do not, the state which realizes them will include subjects for whom the state's authority provides no reason for action, and this must undermine any grounding for political obligations on the part of such subjects. Thus we reach the result that any state which can lay claim to the allegiance of its subjects must present itself to them as informed by a fundamental right of respect.

This is perhaps a rather weak defence of the rationality of a right of respect. At the most, it might be objected, it is only an argument for *speaking of* respect, not for actually *showing* respect. And it must be conceded that nothing here rules out the rationality of ideologies which mask effectively a failure to respect some groups of people; though such ideologies are the tribute that false currency pays to true coin, revealing in their presentation the dialectical rationality of the right of respect. However, once it is conceded that a cautious and prudent egoism which does not require universal respect for others is not an intrinsically incoherent course of action, I do not see how this result could be avoided. The most one can say is that once the dialectical rationality of a right of respect is conceded, for appropriate contexts of discourse, then given reasonable publicity, there will be strong prudential reasons for agents to conform their actions in those contexts to the right of respect.

A further objection is that, on this approach, the rationality of the fundamental right of respect is relative to contexts of discourse – those in which reasons for action are being proffered which are intended to appeal to anyone. Contexts of this kind will typically be ones in which there is some practical project which can only be accomplished successfully with the co-operation of others, who cannot be simply coerced to co-operate; their compliance is needed, and can only be obtained by providing them with reasons for doing so. Obviously, that the proffered reasons satisfy the fundamental right of respect is not likely to be by itself sufficient to secure compliance; my claim is only that it is necessary. But are there any contexts of this kind? I take it to be an important, though contingent, presupposition of modern political theory that there are. That is, first, that many of the ends that people care about can only be achieved with the co-operation of others: and, secondly, that this co-operation often cannot be coerced. This second claim needs more discussion than I can give here, and there certainly appear to have been societies which have relied very greatly on coercion (e.g. ancient Sparta). So I do not want to make any universal claims for the applicability of the dialectical rationality of the right of respect. All I do maintain is that if one reflects on, say, the methods of production and distribution of modern European societies, one will acknowledge the limits of coercion, and thus the applicability to us of the argument for the dialectical rationality of the right of respect.

Having brought this problem to the surface, I want to leave the matter there, and return to the right of freedom. If we now take it that the standard of rationality here is to be that of dialectical rationality, the issue is that of to what freedom a right is derivable, given contingent facts about human needs and desires, from the fundamental right of respect. As I observed before, the freedom (if any) to which we have a right cannot be specified without a full specification of our other rights. It is easy enough to satisfy oneself that a right of respect will yield negative rights to life, limbs, and absence of avoidable suffering. What is much less clear is whether any positive rights of these kinds, and property rights, are thus derivable. Since I do not want to enter into these issues, the full specification of any right to freedom is to that extent unclear. None the less, it seems clear that a right to freedom is thus derivable. For given our manifest interest in our ability to determine important features of our lives as we ourselves choose (e.g. where to live, what occupation to try to pursue, whether to marry, whether to have children, etc. – cf. J. S. Mill *On Liberty* ch. III), respect for another requires that we should not interfere with those of his actions which do not violate anyone's rights. What he is free to do (because not under a duty not to do), respect for him requires of us that we should not prevent him from doing, i.e. that we should recognize that he has a claim-right to do.

This right to freedom is, unsurprisingly enough, a right to 'rightful freedom', as I defined it in the previous part of this paper. Is this a right to 'natural freedom', in Locke's sense? It would be surprising if it were, for since the proper context in which the dialectical rationality of a fundamental right of respect is defensible is that of political debate, it would be strange if one could derive from this right a right to a freedom from all political authority. For this would seem to take one outside the context within which the rationality of the right to that freedom is defensible.

It may seem that this argument is unfair to anarchists: for why should they not be permitted to press their cases within the political forum? The reply is that they are not here excluded; obviously, they can put their case within the context of political debate. What is excluded, however, is that they can claim an intrinsically more cogent position by virtue of their appeal to a right only to natural freedom. For there is nothing in the context of political debate to make this right inherently more rational than a right to a freedom which does not construe all political authority as a constraint on freedom, but regards instead the right to freedom as most plausibly realized within a minimally intrusive system of political authority that defines and protects individual rights.

Once one accepts that our right to freedom is not a right to natural freedom one has to drop the thought that all political authority rests upon consent, at least in the sense in which Locke propounded this thought. This may be held to be no bad thing, given the inherent implausibility of Locke's doctrine. However, Locke's doctrine does point, albeit rather hesitatingly, in the direction of democratic politics.[23] And the issue with which I want to close is whether the account of the right to rightful freedom, and the associated defence of this right as dialectically rational, which I have been exploring, provides the basis for any roughly democratic political rights at all.

The clearest denial of any connection here is provided by Berlin in his essay 'Two Concepts of Liberty'.[24] For among the many, and not obviously uniform, ways in which Berlin seeks to contrast 'negative' and 'positive' freedoms, the predominant contrast appears to be that negative freedom is what I have called rightful freedom, whereas positive freedom is the right to have some say in the government of one's state. And since Berlin emphasizes the contrast between these freedoms, he is committed to a denial of any inherent connection between rightful freedom and democratic rights. He makes this denial explicitly:

> Freedom in this sense [sc. negative] is not, at any rate logically, connected with democracy or self-government. Self-government may, on the whole, provide a better guarantee of the preservation of civil liberties than other regimes, and has been defended as such by libertarians. But there is no necessary connexion between individual liberty and democratic rule. The answer to the question 'Who governs me?' is logically distinct from the question 'How far does government interfere with

me?' It is in this difference that the great contrast between the two concepts of negative and positive liberty, in the end, consists.[25]

In one respect, Berlin's claim here seems undeniable: namely, that in practice there have been undemocratic governments which have protected the freedom and other ordinary rights of their subjects better than many democratic governments. He instances the Prussia of Frederick the Great and the Austria of Josef II;[26] Uganda under British colonial rule provides another plausible instance. None the less, I want to argue that there is a connection here, in that the justification for acknowledging a right to freedom at all also issues in a justification for democratic rights: that one cannot regard the right to freedom as rational without also regarding democratic rights as similarly rational, even though it is possible to enjoy the former without the latter. The argument for this claim goes back to the dialectical rationality of the right to freedom. If it is the context of political debate, of practical discussion, of the offering of reasons for action, that rationally requires respect for a right to freedom, then, surely, such a context also yields as a rational requirement respect for a right to participate in the political process. For what is it to engage in practical discussions with others if not to treat one's audience as beings whose views one is prepared to take account of before acting oneself? Practical discussion is not the issuing, and acceptance, of orders; it takes place precisely where a coercive authority is not dominant, and presupposes a readiness to respond to the views of others by modifying plans if they offer good objections to a proposed course of action. In this way, therefore, the grounds for supposing that the right to freedom is owed to us as rational beings are also grounds for supposing that we have a right to participate in the decision-making procedures of our own state.

The outcome of this argument is a right of participation; and it seems to me a virtue of this approach that it does not try to present the exercise of democratic rights either as some form of consent (Locke) or as the imposition on oneself of an obligation one would not otherwise bear (Rousseau). For neither of these accounts of the exercise of democratic rights make much sense of the situation of one who is in a minority where a majority rule procedure is operative. Does such a person consent to the law he has voted against? Does he impose this law upon himself by voting against it? Of course, there are many manoeuvres that can be made to save appearances at this point; but I know none that are persuasive.

By taking a right to participate in the decision-making pro-cedures of one's state, and not the need for consent, as the basis of democratic rights, this approach avoids these difficulties. Admittedly it does so by making a weaker claim on behalf of individual citizens. One who participates in a debate may be outvoted in the end even though he feels that he has the best of the arguments. But that is an inescapable feature of practical discussions, however rationally conducted. We may hope for agreement; but we can neither expect nor demand it. What we can demand is sufficient respect from others that they should listen to our views, allow us to hear theirs, treat our arguments seriously, permit themselves to be corrected by us, and so on. It is this rational demand that is the basis of our democratic rights.

At this point we can return to the topic of toleration and its justification. A right of participation places on fellow citizens a duty to permit such participation; and this permission is in-separable from toleration of the expression of, and indeed emphatic presentation of, political positions other than one's own. Thus toleration of political dissent should not be regarded as simply arising from respect for our right to freedom. This right yields some justification for political toleration, but only as much as it yields for any form of harmless behaviour; and since political dissent sometimes threatens rights (e.g. property and freedom), the toleration justifiable on this ground alone is potentially rather limited. A defence of political toleration by reference to our right to freedom alone abstracts from the political content of the acts to be tolerated. By contrast, once the demand for political toleration is grounded on an explicitly political right, the right to participate, then that toleration is much more securely established. For if, as I have argued, a right to participate is intrinsic to the possession of any rights at all, then the defence of that right, and the correlated duty of political toleration, acquires a significance which no argument from our right to freedom can provide.

Notes

1 First published in 1690. All my references are to the revised edition by P. Laslett, Cambridge, 1963.
2 ibid., II, 209.
3 ibid., I, 3.
4 ibid., II, 22.
5 ibid., II, 61.
6 ibid., II, 6.
7 Both these views about the connection between reason and natural law look problematic from the perspective of Locke's *Essay*, but I shall not pursue this matter.
8 For details of this dispute, cf. Laslett's introduction to his edition, op. cit., n. 1.
9 op. cit., II, 131.
10 ibid., II, 57.
11 ibid., II, 57.
12 I discuss the issue as to whether there are two concepts of freedom, 'positive' and 'negative', in a paper 'MacCallum and the two concepts of freedom', forthcoming in *Ratio*.
13 op. cit., II, 57.
14 ibid., II, 6.
15 cf. *Essay*, book IV, ch. 3, section 18, and also Locke's early *Essays on the Laws of Nature*, ed. W. Von Leyden, Oxford, 1954, esp. 199–201, and also Von Leyden's introduction, 54–7.
16 I first learned this point from André Gombay. For a good discussion of it, cf. T. Nagel, 'The fragmentation of value', in his *Mortal Questions*, Cambridge, 1979.
17 cf. R. M. Hare, *Moral Thinking*, Oxford, 1981.
18 cf. J. L. Mackie, *Ethics*, Harmondsworth, 1977, 96–7.
19 G. W. F. Hegel, *The Phenomenology of Mind*, trans. J. M. Baillie, rev. edn, London, 1931, 229–40.
20 J. P. Sartre, *Critique of Dialectical Reason*, trans. A. Sheridan-Smith, London, 1976, 158, n. 37.
21 T. H. Green, *Prolegomena to Ethics*, Oxford, 1883, 210.
22 H. Sidgwick, *Lectures on Green, Spencer, and Martineau*, London, 1902, 66–7.
23 For an excellent account of the place of consent in Locke's political

theory, cf. J. Dunn, 'Consent in the political theory of John Locke', *The Historical Journal*, 10, 1967.

24 This essay is reprinted in I. Berlin, *Four Essays on Liberty*, Oxford, 1969, and my references are to this edition of it.

25 ibid., 129–30.

26 ibid., 129, n. 3.

3

Repressive toleration revisited: Mill, Marcuse, MacIntyre

ALEX CALLINICOS

Because Mill was so ambivalent in his sense of what an individual actually amounted to, he could not base his defence of a right to tolerance on any strong concept of individual personality and what aspects of this might be judged to deserve respect. Instead he was obliged to weave nervously together a reasonably plausible argument taken from his philosophy of science about the conditions for developing rational understanding, a strikingly implausible general theory of social change and a decidedly Romantic conception of the cultural mission of the resolutely unpopular, especially among the intelligentsia.[1]

John Dunn's elegant formulation admirably summarizes some of the tensions in Mill's thoughts on liberty. It comes as some surprise, however, to turn to Herbert Marcuse's 'Repressive Tolerance', and to find there precisely the same themes attributed by Dunn to Mill – an account of rationality, a conception of change which focuses on the role of ideas, and a stress on the progressive role of enlightened but embattled minorities. This discovery is surprising because Marcuse draws a conclusion starkly opposed to Mill's. Notoriously, Marcuse denounces the 'abstract' or 'false' tolerance which permits the expression of any opinion, and argues for 'liberating tolerance', which 'would mean intolerance against movements from the Right, and toleration of movements from the Left' (109).[2]

The issues raised by Marcuse are important in three respects. First, from a purely historical point of view, his arguments had an important influence upon the American New Left in the late 1960s, and played some part in persuading them to move beyond a comparatively traditional liberal defence of certain rights (as evidenced, for example, by the very name of the Berkeley Free Speech Movement in 1964), and peaceful opposition to the Vietnam war, to increasingly violent confrontation with the state. One has to be careful, however, not to fall into Marcuse's trap of overestimating the influence of intellectuals on political events; one does not have to look much further than Mayor Daley of Chicago for an explanation of the Weathermen. Furthermore, Marcuse never endorsed terrorism as a political strategy in the advanced capitalist countries, and strongly condemned such actions as the assassination of Hans-Martin Schleyer by the Red Army Faction in his native Germany.

Secondly, Mill so strongly insists on the connection between rationality and toleration in *On Liberty* that it is worth considering arguments which start from similar premises (especially the internal connection between freedom and reason), but draw different conclusions. This essay will concentrate on examining the arguments of this nature offered by Marcuse. Although I shall claim that he does not succeed in making out his case, his attempt to do so does not deserve the cavalier and crushing dismissal that it has received, for example, at the hands of Alasdair MacIntyre.[3] Given, however, the force and clarity of MacIntyre's critique, I have inevitably paid considerable attention to his arguments.

Thirdly, the question of the precise limits, if any, which should be set to the free expression of opinions is a matter of some political importance in contemporary Britain. The emergence of fascist movements, such as the National Front, which use the incitement of racial hatred as a means of winning popular support has led both to calls for their suppression by the state and to attempts to prevent them from marching and holding meetings by the Anti-Nazi League and similar organizations.[4] Since I agree with the view that fascists should be denied a public platform, yet reject the arguments which Marcuse offers to justify such a view, it is incumbent on me to provide some of my own, which I do at the end of this essay.

54

Before going on actually to consider Marcuse's argument I should say first that one of the great difficulties with 'Repressive Tolerance' is to establish what this argument is. The reader is confronted with a medley of different claims jumbled together, to do, for example, with the fake objectivity of the mass media, the essential role of violence in achieving social progress, and so on. Marcuse may have two reasons for this confusing approach, one good, and one bad. The good reason is that one cannot separate the question of toleration from more general issues concerning the nature of society, and the conditions under which social justice may be attained. In other words, Marcuse, to some degree, makes a discussion of tolerance the pretext of a broader critique of contemporary society.

The bad reason is to do with Marcuse's frequently expressed disdain of what he called formal logic. The law of contradiction, according to Marcuse, involves the denial that there may be conflicts within reality itself, and is thus part of the 'technological rationality' of late capitalism.[5] I shall not waste any time with absurdities of this sort since MacIntyre has made short, and devastating, work of them.[6]

Fortunately, Marcuse's practice is better than his theory. It is possible to identify an argument running through 'Repressive Tolerance', and to cast it into a deductive form. The argument involves the following:

1 A major premiss setting out a claim concerning what Marcuse calls 'the internal connection between liberty and truth' (86).

2 A minor premiss asserting that the conditions of modern industrial society involve the effective suppression of freedom as conceived in terms of 1.

3 A conclusion to the effect that the attainment of the freedom denied under present conditions requires toleration of the left and suppression of the right.

I shall argue, first, that while the major premiss may, if correctly interpreted, be true, it would not support the conclusion, even if the minor premiss were true, and, secondly, that the minor premiss is in any case false, at least in the extreme version of it given by Marcuse.

Let us now consider Marcuse's argument in detail. He writes:

Liberty is self-determination, autonomy – this is almost a tautology, but a tautology which results from a whole series of synthetic judgments. It stipulates the ability to determine one's own life: to be able to determine what to do and what not to do, what to suffer and what not. But the subject is never the contingent, private individual as that which he actually is or happens to be; it is rather the individual as a human being who is capable of being free with the others (86–7).

Marcuse's is thus, in the terms popularized by Isaiah Berlin, a positive concept of freedom. That is, it is concerned less with the degree to which individual agents are left to pursue their wants without interference from or regulation by the state, but rather on their *capacity* to arrive at some rational assessment of what these wants should be and how they may be realized.

The necessary connection between freedom thus conceived and rationality is made explicit in the following passage:

Tolerance of free speech is the way of improvement, of progress in liberation, *not* because there is no objective truth, and improvement must necessarily be a compromise between a variety of opinions, but because there *is* an objective truth which can be discovered, ascertained only in learning and comprehending that which is and that which can and ought to be done for the sake of improving the lot of mankind. This common and historical 'ought' is not immediately evident, at hand: it has to be uncovered by 'cutting through', 'splitting', 'breaking asunder' (*dis-cutio*) the given material – separating right and wrong, good and bad, correct and incorrect. (89–90)

Marcuse here is arguing that, even in Mill, 'the telos of tolerance is truth' (90). In doing so, however, he offers an account of reason which focuses, not as Mill and the analytic tradition (which in this respect at least shares his sympathies) would, on the formal procedures through which beliefs are subjected to critical examination, but on the tensions within reality which thought seeks to uncover. Much fuller versions of this account are provided by Marcuse in his essays of the 1930s, some of which have been collected in English under the title of *Negations*, and in *Reason and*

Revolution (1941). There he champions the virtues of a philosophical tradition beginning with Plato and Aristotle and culminating in Hegel and Marx, whose starting point is the contradiction between appearance and essence, and therefore the falsity of *doxa*, of those beliefs which merely record the deliverance of observation. Genuine knowledge depends on penetrating beneath the appearances to the underlying reality. Consequently, reason is necessarily negative and critical, since it refuses to take the appearances at their face value, and is destructive of *doxa*. Hence also the potentially subversive nature of reason, since by highlighting the contrast between appearance and essence it reveals the basis of class society on poverty and exploitation, and points towards a liberated society, in which opposites have been reconciled and harmonized.

Two things are worth noting about this account of reason. The first is that what Marcuse regards as the structural properties of rationality, above all its constant penetrating beneath the appearances to the essence, provide it with a potentially critical and revolutionary content. This helps to fill out what Marcuse means by saying that 'the telos of tolerance is truth'. Truth is not a property of sentences, it is a real condition towards which we strive, the liberated society of the future. Secondly, Marcuse's is a monologic concept of reason. Compare Mill's defence of freedom of opinion in chapter II of *On Liberty*. The telos of tolerance is truth here also, but because of the essential role of free discussion in permitting us to distinguish between true and false assertions, and to hold our beliefs on rational grounds, rather than on the basis of unreflective tradition. Marcuse, however, in the passage cited above treats discussion, not as a relation between speakers, but as the action of thought on the reality which it seeks to split into essence and appearance. This is a view of reason which sets Marcuse apart, not only from Mill, but also from critical theorists such as Habermas, who seeks to elucidate the structure of rationality by analysing the 'ideal speech-situation' implicit in every utterance, an approach which necessarily conceives reason as dialogic, based on a community of speakers.[7]

We can bring out the relevance of these considerations to the question of tolerance by reminding ourselves that freedom for Marcuse is *self*-determination, and that this self is not 'the

57

contingent, private individual', but the *rational* subject, able critically to analyse his social and natural environment, and to transform it in the light of this analysis. But what happens when contingent individuals are prevented from fulfilling their potential as rational agents?

This is the burden of Marcuse's critique of Mill:

> Even the all-inclusive character of liberalist [*sic*] tolerance was, at least in theory, based on the proposition that men were (potential) individuals, who could learn to hear and see and feel by themselves, to develop their own thoughts, to grasp their true interests and rights and capabilities, also against established authority and opinion. This was the rationale of free speech and assembly. Universal toleration becomes questionable when its rationale no longer prevails, when tolerance is administered to manipulated and indoctrinated individuals who parrot, as their own, the opinions of their masters, for whom heteronomy has become autonomy. (90)

It is here that 'Repressive Tolerance' converges with *One-Dimensional Man*. For the minor premiss of Marcuse's argument against tolerance is that the structure of the 'totally administered societies' of the West is such as to suppress the overwhelming majority's reasoning powers. *One-Dimensional Man* is his most extended attempt to make out this claim; in turn it draws heavily on three of the great classics of Frankfurt Marxism, Horkheimer and Adorno's *Dialectic of Enlightenment*, Horkheimer's *Eclipse of Reason* and Adorno's *Minima Moralia*.[8]

The Frankfurt School's claim is the very strong one that it is no longer possible to talk about individual *agents* any longer. The sheer productivity and economic dynamism of late capitalism make it possible to penetrate the inner world of the individual's mental life, and to shape his or her conscious and unconscious desires.

This is the central significance of Marcuse's celebrated discussion of 'false needs', 'which are superimposed upon the individual by particular social interests in his repression', and which include 'most of the prevailing needs to relax, to have fun, to behave and consume in accordance with the advertisements, to love and hate what others love and hate':

Their satisfaction might be most gratifying to the individual but this condition is not a condition which has to be maintained and protected if it serves to arrest the development of the ability (his own and others) to recognise the disease of the whole and grasp the chances of curing the disease. The result then is euphoria in unhappiness.[9]

The generation of false needs by consumer capitalism means that individuals are 'incapable of being autonomous'.[10] The relation between individual and society is not even that of a pragmatic adjustment to an independently existing reality; rather that reality cracked the individual open, penetrated the inner recesses of his mind, so that he merely reflects and reproduces the total structure of society. 'The result is, not adjustment but *mimesis*: an immediate identification of the individual with *his* society and, through it, with the society as a whole.'[11]

The implication of this analysis for the issue of tolerance is as follows. Since people are prevented from realizing their potential as rational agents, the conditions on which the 'liberalist tolerance' defended by Mill depended no longer exist. Indeed, the 'abstract tolerance' of all opinions characteristic of Western liberal democracies represents the transformation of what was once a progressive and revolutionary demand into a prop of an irrational social order. Much of 'Repressive Tolerance' is devoted to this favourite theme of Marcuse, already well-represented in his writings of the 1930s: liberalism, from being the revolutionary ideology of opposition to the feudal *ancien régime* has become a rationalization of the effectively totalitarian social order of late capitalism.[12] Thus Marcuse argues that tolerance has become a rhetoric which conceals the suppression of 'effective dissent', less through physical repression than through the formation, by means of 'monopolistic media', of 'a mentality ... for which right and wrong, true or false are predefined wherever they affect the vital interests of the society' (95). This situation can be redressed, people's capacity to reason reawakened, only through 'the systematic withdrawal of tolerance from regressive and repressive opinions and movements' (101). Thus, in a satisfactorily dialectical fashion, the internal connection between freedom and truth now requires, not toleration, but intolerance.

Before I go on to criticize this argument, let me say something about its virtues. First, if we take the fact of diversity to be one premiss of any argument for toleration,[13] then we should note that Marcuse's is not an argument for the suppression of diversity. Indeed, one of the chief complaints of the Frankfurt School against contemporary society is that they see it as one which systematically destroys diversity, transforming individuals into qualitatively identical rnits of a homogenized and uniform sociality. This is especially noteworthy in Adorno's writings,[14] but is also true of Marcuse. It is to be found, for example, in his discussions of the role of art as a critical and revolutionary force, and in his championing of the progressive role of minorities.[15] No more than Marx himself is he vulnerable to the vulgar criticism that his aim is the suppression of difference, the imposition of a closed society. His criticism of the totally administered society he saw around him is precisely that it is such a closed society.

Secondly, there seems to me little doubt that Marcuse correctly identified a common feature of political behaviour in advanced capitalist societies, namely that the 'extremes' of right and left, while usually not physically suppressed (although we should not forget such practices as the West German *Berufsverbot*), are effectively excluded from the terms of political debate in public forums. Nor can one quarrel much with his attack on the debased character of this discussion. The 1983 general election marked a low point in British political debate. Much of the mass media heaped adulation on a politician whose policies would have been rejected as extremist a few years earlier, connived to conceal the manifest difficulties her government was in, and hurled scurrilous abuse at her opponents. Plenty of research has been done, partly thanks to Marcuse's inspiration, into the way in which public discussion is managed and manipulated. We may question his explanation of this phenomenon, and argue that he has overstated its effects, but it is difficult in good faith to deny its existence, and to the extent that Marcuse alerted us to the scale of the problem, he is entitled to our gratitude.

Thirdly, Marcuse's denunciation of 'false tolerance' is a useful corrective to some of the less attractive features of contemporary academic life. In the social sciences at least, the willingness to listen, and to give consideration to a variety of opinions sometimes

60

hardens into a vulgar sort of Weberianism, in which debate is actually avoided on the grounds that, so it is claimed, rational procedures for settling theoretical disputes do not exist, and that therefore the best we can do is agree to differ. Marcuse's insistence that tolerance is important, not because it permits a mart of paradigms between which one can freely choose, but because of the relation it may have to establishing the truth of certain theories and the falsity of others, seems to me both healthy and right. It is also a matter in which he is in full agreement with Mill and Popper.

The relationship between tolerance, rationality and freedom is indeed the first of the issues which I wish to consider in criticizing Marcuse's argument against intolerance. It is perhaps the chief object of MacIntyre's attack on 'Repressive Tolerance':

> The telos of tolerance is not truth, but rationality. Certainly we value rationality because it is by rational methods that we discover truth; but a man may be rational who holds many false beliefs, and a man may have true beliefs and yet be irrational. What is crucial is that the former has the possibility of progressing towards truth, while the second not only has no grounds for asserting what he believes, even though it is true, but is continually liable to acquire false beliefs. What is it to be rational? It is a necessary condition of rationality that a man shall formulate his beliefs in such a way that it is clear what evidence would be evidence *against* them, and that he shall himself be open to criticism and refutation in the light of any possible objection. But to foreclose on tolerance is precisely to cut oneself off from such criticism and refutation. It is to gravely endanger one's own rationality by not admitting one's own fallibility.[16]

Note that MacIntyre is not denying that there is any connection between tolerance and truth. Rather, his argument is that our hopes for attaining the truth depend on the existence of tolerance. For it is only by granting freedom of opinion that the process of conjecture and refutation through which false beliefs are rejected and true(r) beliefs adopted can flourish. This conception of rationality is, of course, Popper's, but it is also present in *On Liberty* and has been taken much further by more recent philosophers of science such as Feyerabend and Lakatos, who claim that scientific progress depends on theoretical pluralism, i.e the existence of competing research programmes.

It is not clear how Marcuse would reply to this argument. His account of reason does not free him from the obligation to say under what conditions beliefs should be rejected or accepted. Unfortunately, Marcuse's hopelessly misguided rejection of logic and of the empirical procedures of the natural sciences means that he does not fulfil this obligation.

One could, however, reply to MacIntyre on Marcuse's behalf that, granted the necessary connection of rationality to toleration, the structure of society is such as to prevent agents from being rational. The virtues of tolerance have been rendered wholly theoretical by the capture of our minds by late capitalism.

Here we run into the straightforwardly empirical question of the merits of the Frankfurt School's analysis of the relation between individual and society in the advanced capitalist societies. One does not have to be an apologist for these societies to argue that the analysis is false. To make out the account of false needs in *One-Dimensional Man* involves, at the very least, the claim that the advanced liberal democracies rest upon the normative integration of their citizens – in other words, the existence of a set of beliefs about society shared by all its members which leads them to accept its legitimacy. There are strong empirical and conceptual grounds for doubting that such a claim is true.[17] Moreover, a persuasive argument has been made out to the effect that societies depend on normative integration far less than they do on the cruder but no less effective mechanisms of economic compulsion and physical coercion. The typical attitude of the individual towards his or her society is more likely to be pragmatic acceptance than wholesale rejection or the complete indoctrination which Marcuse is so ready to attribute to the Western working class.[18]

But even if Marcuse's theory of false needs were correct, it is not obvious how a strategy of 'liberating tolerance' which suppresses the opinions of the right is going to remedy the situation. For example, precisely which opinions are to be denied toleration? Marcuse sometimes casts his net very wide indeed, advocating

> the withdrawal of toleration of speech and assembly from
> groups and movements which promote aggressive policies,

armament, chauvinism, discrimination on the grounds of race or religion, or which oppose the extension of public services, social security, medical care, etc. Moreover, the restoration of freedom of thought may necessitate new and rigid restrictions on teachings and practices in the educational institutions which, by their very methods and concepts, serve to enclose the mind within the established universe of discourse and behaviour – thereby precluding *a priori* rational evaluation of the alternatives. (100–1)

When 'Repressive Tolerance' first appeared, in 1965, such an all-inclusive approach would have implied the suppression of both major political parties in the United States and Britain (not to speak of the closure of most Philosophy departments in the English-speaking world, the target of the concluding sentence of the passage just quoted).

The wide scope of 'liberating tolerance' obviously raises the question of who on earth will actually carry out this programme. This issue in turn is connected to the difficult matter of the agency of change in Marcuse's version of socialism. Here he is at his most vague and equivocal. Notoriously, Marcuse held that the industrial working class has become integrated into the structure of capitalism, and so cannot play the revolutionary role ascribed to it by classical Marxism: 'in the absence of agents and agencies of social change, ... there is no ground on which theory and practice, thought and action meet'.[19] It is, however, equally well known that Marcuse believed there to be minorities which could to some degree substitute for the proletariat. *One-Dimensional Man* concludes with a celebrated invocation of 'the outcasts and outsiders, the exploited and persecuted or other races and other colours, the unemployed and the unemployable'.[20]

Marcuse's most careful (the term is relative) discussion of the problem is in his *Essay on Liberation*, written shortly before the French events of May–June 1968.[21] Here, he insists both that 'the working class is still the historical agent of revolution', and that 'it has become a conservative, even counter-revolutionary force'.[22] His focus is on the 'potential catalysts of rebellion', namely 'the militant intelligentsia' and 'the ghetto population'.[23]

This line of thought raises the question of whether MacIntyre is right to argue that:

Marcuse ... has taken over from liberal and right-wing critics of the European revolutionary tradition a theory which they falsely ascribed to the left, but which was rarely held until Marcuse espoused it. Both the Jacobins and Lenin believed in a temporary dictatorship of the majority over counter-revolutionary minorities – whatever they may have practised. But it was left to Marcuse to profess a belief in a dictatorship by a minority.[24]

Certainly, Marcuse sometimes seems to express such a belief. Thus, he suggests that the creation of false needs has led to a

> stage where people cannot reject the system of domination without rejecting themselves, their own repressive instinctual needs and values. We would have to conclude that liberation would mean subversion against the will and against the prevailing interests of the great majority of the people.[25]

Perhaps in part to *épater les bourgeois*, Marcuse sometimes invokes Mill's support for the notion of a 'democratic educational dictatorship of free men'. The argument seems to be that self-determination is only possible if one 'has learned to think rationally and autonomously', and that 'where society has entered the phase of total administration and indoctrination, this would be a small number indeed, and not necessarily that of the elected representatives of the people' (106).

But Marcuse always pulls back from the brink. For example, after citing Mill's advocacy of plural voting in *Considerations on Representative Government*, he concludes, 'however, the alternative to the established semi-democratic process is *not* a dictatorship or élite, no matter how intellectual and intelligent, but the struggle for a real democracy' (122). This struggle will be the work of 'radical minorities ... – minorities intolerant, militantly intolerant and disobedient to the rules of behaviour which tolerate destruction and suppression' (123). Marcuse certainly resembles Mill in having 'a decidedly Romantic conception of the cultural mission of the resolutely unpopular, especially among the intelligentsia'.

One puzzle about 'Repressive Tolerance' is whether the 'practice of discriminating tolerance' (123) involves merely vocal opposition to, rather than the active suppression of, reactionary opinions and movements. It is impossible to read Marcuse's essay without wondering whether he is guilty of an equivocation between two senses of tolerance. In the first sense, to tolerate someone's opinion or actions is to acquiesce in them, irrespective of whether we have the power to stop them. Thus, in this sense, I might refuse to tolerate government defence policy without there being any suggestion that I either can or wish to prevent that policy being implemented, otherwise than through not voting Conservative in the next election. In the second sense, to tolerate someone's actions or opinions is not to impede their doing or expression, even if we have the power to do so, and strongly disapprove of them. It is surely this second sense of toleration that is advocated by Mill and his heirs, and that is relevant to the discussion of free speech.[26]

The fuzziness of Marcuse's use of the terms 'toleration' and 'tolerance' is related to his infuriating tendency to mix into his critique of 'abstract tolerance' discussions of the legitimacy of civil disobedience, and of revolutionary violence (e.g. 106–9). The danger of such conceptual insouciance is that one might take the argument for 'discriminating tolerance' which I have been discussing to justify the systematic use of violence by 'radical minorities' in order to impose a new form of society 'against the will and against the prevailing interests of the great majority of the people'.

This suggests that, while, as I noted at the beginning of this paper, Marcuse disassociated himself from the use of political terrorism by some left-wing groups, he cannot be wholly exculpated from the disastrous consequences of the actions of the Red Brigades, Red Army Faction, and other such organizations. He writes, for example, of the role of vanguard actions by revolutionary minorities in the 'radical enlightenment' of the masses, and of the collapse of 'the traditional distinction between legitimate and illegitimate violence'.[27] No wonder that some of his readers may have concluded that it was up to them to galvanize the working class out of their indoctrinated slumbers by means of the bullet and the bomb. The effect on the Italian left especially has been little short of catastrophic.[28]

Underlying Marcuse's equivocation is a deep misunderstanding of the nature of freedom. For if 'liberty is self-determination', then it is difficult to see how one might acquire the capacity to think and behave autonomously except through beginning to exercise that capacity. Or, as Hegel put it, one cannot learn to swim without getting into the water. This is not to suggest that learning is possible without any guidance or teaching. Nevertheless, to suppose, as Marcuse does, that 'the catalysts of transformation operate [to break down the working-class indoctrination] "from without"'[29] is, as Marx put it in the *Theses on Feuerbach*, 'to divide society into two parts, one of which is superior to society'.[30] The revolutionary minority is supposed by Marcuse to be somehow exempt from the social processes which have transformed the mass of the population into a conservative force. The *Theses on Feuerbach* were addressed by Marx against the Utopian socialists and young Hegelians of his day. As MacIntyre notes, there are striking echoes of the Hegelian left in Marcuse's writings.[31] Bruno Bauer, like Marcuse, counterposed critical reason to the dull and indoctrinated masses. (Marcuse's disdain for ordinary people sometimes breaks through, as in the following passage, saturated with the *hauteur* of a central European intellectual, educated in the high culture of pre-Nazi Germany: 'the degree to which the population is allowed to break the peace wherever there is still peace and silence, to be ugly and to uglify things, to ooze familiarity, to offend against good form is frightening'.[32]) Like the young Hegelians, Marcuse underestimated the rationality and commonsense of working people, and correlatively overestimated the power of pure reason to transform society through the actions of 'radical minorities'. It is little wonder that he admired the élitist communism of Babeuf and Blanqui, for example writing the preface to an English translation of Babeuf's trial. The notion central to Marx's own thought that socialism is the *self*-emancipation of the working class is quite absent from his writings. Marcuse's 'general theory of social change' is as 'strikingly implausible' as Mill's.[33]

To conclude this discussion of Marcuse, let me summarize my argument. First, even if we accept Marcuse's major premiss, that there is an internal connection between freedom and truth, the structure of rationality needed if we are to pursue the truth with hopes of more than chance successes requires the toleration of diverse beliefs. Secondly, Marcuse's minor premiss, that the 'totally administered society' prevents people from realizing their potential as rational agents, is false. Thirdly, his conclusion that tolerance is incompatible with the restoration to people of their rational potential, does not follow from these premisses, and is expounded in so confused a way as to license, on some readings, political terrorism and minority dictatorship. We must, therefore, account 'Repressive Tolerance' a failure. Moreover, since the essay highlights central problems concerning Marcuse's analysis of contemporary capitalism and his strategy for change, we can only conclude that his political thought as a whole is fatally flawed. This is not to ignore the personal courage and intellectual intransigence of Marcuse's lonely fight against the reigning Western orthodoxies of the 1950s and 1960s. However, his importance as a philosopher lies not in his political writings but elsewhere, for example in his discussion of aesthetic questions.

There is, however, a sting in this essay's tail. While Marcuse's argument against intolerance is a bad one, it does not follow that there are *no* good arguments for preventing the expression of certain opinions. The case I have in mind is that of fascist movements. 'Fascism' in my usage is not a generic term for any right-wing political grouping. Rather, it refers to a specific form of capitalist political rule, one which, unlike parliamentary democracy, does not seek to incorporate working-class organizations within the framework of the polity, but instead systematically destroys them. Fascist movements seek to install such a form of state by mobilizing the lower middle classes around a programme which combines plebeian anti-capitalism, extreme nationalism and racism, and the organization of direct action against their enemies – the left, the trade unions, racial minorities.

The classic version of this conception of fascism was that developed by Leon Trotsky in his brilliant analysis of Hitler's rise to power in Germany. His was a dynamic account, explaining the growth of fascism as the response of certain classes (above all big business and the petty bourgeoisie) to conditions of acute economic and political crisis which rendered parliamentary democracy no longer viable:

At the moment when the 'normal' police and military resources of the bourgeois dictatorship, together with their parliamentary screens, no longer suffice to hold society in a state of equilibrium – the turn of the fascist regime arrives. Through the fascist agency, capitalism sets in motion the masses of the crazed petty bourgeoisie, and bands of de-classed and demoralised *Lumpenproletariat*; all the countless human beings whom finance capital has itself brought to desperation and frenzy. From fascism the bourgeoisie demands a thorough job; once it has resorted to the methods of civil war, it insists on having peace for a period of years. And the fascist agency by utilising the petty bourgeoisie as a battering ram, by overturning all obstacles in its path, does a thorough job.... When a state turns fascist ... it means, first of all for the most part, that the workers' organisations are annihilated; that the proletariat is reduced to an amorphous state; and that a system of administration is created which penetrates deeply into the masses and which serves to frustrate the independent crystallisation of the proletariat. Therein precisely is the gist of fascism.[34]

Now while no Western society since 1945 has experienced a crisis on the scale of that suffered by Germany between the wars, there do exist a number of classical fascist movements in the advanced industrial countries. The dominant organization on the British extreme right is the National Front, whose leaders have always modelled themselves on the German Nazis, and which was taken over at the end of 1983 by a group influenced by the examples of Gregor Strasser's 'social' fascism, and of the terrorist 'strategy of tension' pursued by Italian fascists since the late 1960s. The British fascists' anti-semitic and violent proclivities, and their international connections, are regularly documented by the admirable anti-racist magazine *Searchlight*. I believe most strongly that the National Front and its like should be denied the normal rights of free speech and assembly.

My reasons for doing so are not concerned primarily with the *content* of the British Nazis' beliefs. It is difficult to imagine a more evil doctrine than one which aspires to emulate Hitler. In itself, however, this does not constitute grounds for suppressing those who accept such a doctrine. Much of what the present British government does and says is, in my view, immoral, but I do not therefore advocate the application of 'discriminating tolerance' to Mrs Thatcher, for the little that would be worth. Nor is it a matter of fascist doctrines giving offence to black and Jewish people, although this is often invoked as grounds for preventing Nazi marches from taking place, especially in what are still quaintly known as immigrant areas. My argument favours no platform for *fascists*, as opposed to what is sometimes proposed, no platform for racists, a much broader net which could plausibly include a wide spectrum of the mainstream political parties as well as theorists of genetic differences in intelligence such as Eysenck.

A study of fascist parties in Britain reveals that their meetings and marches are not concerned chiefly to expose their views to the public eye. (Indeed, during the NF's period of electoral success in the mid-1970s, it was extremely difficult to elicit its leaders' beliefs on such matters as close to their hearts as their long-held hatred of Jewish people.) Primarily, the public activities of the fascist parties are displays of strength and incitements to racial violence. This is reflected not simply in the format of the marches – the phalanx of Union Jacks on spears at the head, the Honour Guard of thugs surrounding the mini-führer, and so on. It is also manifest in the incidents attendant on such events – the invasion of the area selected for the meeting or march by fascist hooligans, and the attacks which invariably both precede and follow the public event.

My argument is that such violence is a necessary, rather than contingent, feature of fascist movements, that it is through the public display of a potential for organized violence, and the tacit encouragement of racial attacks that they both propagate and win support for their ideas. For the aim of the NF and its like is less to win electoral support (although there have been times when they have gone all-out for such support) than to build an organized mass-following capable of the systematic use of violence against their opponents – black and Jewish people, the trade unions and the left. The incitement to violence now serves both to firm up those who are already members of the fascist parties, and to attract to them others to whom such activities offer one way of giving meaning to an empty life.

Colin Sparks suggests that constant resort to violence arises from the very nature of fascist movements, which weld together diverse social strata, not only the petty bourgeoisie and white-collar workers, but also manual workers and the unemployed, transforming these groups' revulsion from the existing order into an assault on the most serious threat to that order, the organized labour movement. The fascists' characteristic 'stress on action and violence' tends both to impose some form of unity, often a military one, on a socially heterogeneous movement, and to temper it for the bigger confrontations to which its leaders aspire.[35]

The case for suppressing fascist parties is that the propagation of their views is inseparable from the incitement and use of violence. The argument is rather a simple one: it certainly does not raise very profound considerations concerning the nature of freedom and reason of the sort invoked by Marcuse. One does not have to go beyond Mill's text to justify what I have proposed:

> Even opinions lose their immunity when the circumstances in which they are expressed are such as to constitute their expression a positive instigation to some mischievous act. An opinion that corn-dealers are starvers of the poor, or that private property is robbery, ought to be unmolested when simply circulated through the press, but may justly incur punishment when delivered orally to an excited mob assembled before the house of a corn-dealer, or when handed about among the same mob in the form of a placard.[36]

(Like Marcuse, I have succumbed to the temptation of invoking Mill's support for the refusal to tolerate certain views.)

One difficulty the liberal reader may have with this argument is the following. The case of the corn-dealer is one in which the expression of certain beliefs may legitimately be suppressed because of the circumstances of their utterance and the intentions of the speaker. It is a matter of some *individual* action in its specific context. Presumably the form which Mill envisaged suppression should take was that of the subsequent prosecution of the agitator under the criminal law. (Indeed, the common law possesses a formidable battery of offences capable of serving this purpose.) I, on the other hand, am proposing the *general* prohibition of certain political *parties*, on the grounds, less of any specific actions done by them, than of their propensity to encourage a certain class of undesirable actions. The arena has shifted from that of individual subjects and their actions to that of a social phenomenon, namely

70

fascism, with certain inherent characteristics and tendencies.[37]

There is comparatively little I can do to alleviate the unease this surreptitious change of terrain may cause. In my defence I can only claim that the difficulty arises from applying the concepts of liberal political philosophy to the terrors and dramas of our century. This philosophy seeks in different ways to build an account of rational social life starting from the thoughts and doings of individual human agents. Its optimism about individuals' ability to control their circumstances has always rendered this approach rather implausible, though the Victorian 'age of improvement' made things seem otherwise, at least for a minority. World war, the triumphs of fascism and Stalinism in the inter-war years shattered these 'illusions of progress'. A lasting achievement of the Frankfurt School, despite inconsequences and inconsistencies which I have catalogued in Marcuse, was to demonstrate the degree to which the categories of liberal thought simply could not comprehend the world of Hitler and Stalin.

My attempt to apply Mill to the case of fascism is, therefore, more than anything else, a challenge to liberal political philosophers. What has liberalism to say about movements which use the facade of parliament in order to build an order based on violence? How can those concerned to increase the general sum of human welfare deal with regimes which seem at times to be moved by nothing more than the urge to destroy? What sense can a body of thought based on the notion of the individual subject make of social *movements* such as fascism, or indeed of classes, social formations, modes of production and all the other 'natural kinds' which inhabit the human world as surely as other kinds do the physical?

The most sensible liberal response to these rather apocalyptic remarks would be to deflate them. One might concede that the NF and their like have forfeited the *right* to toleration, but still hold that the consequences of actually denying them that right might be so undesirable as to count against suppressing them. Someone of this way of thinking might say that the fascist parties are so insignificant that to act against them would be of little moment, perhaps even winning them sympathy, while constituting a dangerous precedent for the denial of toleration to other, more deserving causes.

71

To see the weakness of this reply we must consider the implications of conceiving fascism as a social phenomenon. From this perspective individual actions fall into a definite, and repeatable, pattern. Fascist movements arise in certain historical conditions, and display a certain dynamic. Many of those conditions are met today – international tensions, mass unemployment, racial conflict. It is true that fascism, in Britain at least, is a marginal political force. So too were the German Nazis until 1929. There was a time in the late 1970s when the NF's electoral successes led serious commentators to predict that they would speedily replace the Liberals as the third party of the realm.[38] A major reason why that particular piece of mould-breaking did not occur was the determined action of the Anti-Nazi League in organizing opposition to the fascists. It would be a mistake to regard the NF's subsequent decline amid a rash of splits with too much complacency. Hitler survived similar setbacks. His own view of the matter, that ruthless action by their opponents could have destroyed the Nazis at their embryonic stage, should surely carry some authority. The recent electoral successes of the Front National in France may serve as a reminder of the potential of contemporary fascism to become more than a lunatic fringe.

The distaste which my proposals will no doubt arouse among many readers is to some degree a function of the relative tranquillity with which Britain has weathered the storms of this century. But this is no justification for supposing that British political culture is permanently immunized against the bacilli of fascism. The point was well made recently by Christopher Ricks in a review of Nicholas Mosley's biography of his father Oswald. Reminding us that a large portion of the British establishment was prepared at least to toy with Mosley in the 1930s, Ricks reports a contemporary *trahison des clercs*:

> The smart thing to do in the New Right of Cambridge lately was to quote (oh of course to quote, not to take the rap for coining) the remark that the real charge against Hitler was that he made an intelligent anti-semitism impossible.[39]

The weakness of Marcuse's arguments should not, therefore, be allowed to obscure the importance of the issues raised by 'Repressive Tolerance'.

Notes

1 J. Dunn, *Western Political Theory in the Face of the Future*, Cambridge, 1979, 53.
2 Citations in the text are from H. Marcuse, 'Repressive Tolerance', in R. P. Wolff *et al.*, *A Critique of Pure Tolerance*, Boston, 1969.
3 A. MacIntyre, *Marcuse*, London, 1970, 89–92.
4 I should stress that, as I explain later, I use the word 'fascist' not as a term of abuse, but as a fairly precise way of characterizing certain political movements and regimes.
5 See, for example, H. Marcuse, *One-Dimensional Man* (hereinafter *ODM*), London, 1968, 115.
6 A. MacIntyre, op. cit., ch. 7.
7 J. Habermas, *Communication and the Evolution of Society*, London, 1979, and *Theory of Communicative Action*, London, 1984. The distinction between monologic and dialogic conceptions of thought derives from Mikhail Bakhtin: see especially V. N. Voloshinov, *Marxism and the Philosophy of Language*, New York, 1973, and M. M. Bakhtin, *The Dialogic Imagination*, Austin, 1981. For an interpretation of Plato which traces his evolution from a dialogic to a monologic view of rationality, see H. Stenzel, *Plato's Method of Dialectic*, New York, 1964.
8 On the emergence of this analysis see M. Jay, *The Dialectical Imagination*, London, 1973.
9 *ODM*, 21–2.
10 ibid, 22.
11 ibid, 25.
12 See, for example, H. Marcuse, 'The struggle against liberalism in the totalitarian view of the state', in *Negations*, Harmondsworth, 1971.
13 See the essay by A. Weale in this volume.
14 See T. W. Adorno, *Minima Moralia*, London, 1974, and *Negative Dialectics*, London, 1973.
15 See especially H. Marcuse, *An Essay on Liberation* (hereinafter *EL*), Harmondsworth, 1972.
16 A. MacIntyre, op. cit., 90–1.
17 M. Mann, 'The social cohesion of liberal democracy', in A. Giddens and D. Held (eds), *Class, Power and Conflict*, London, 1982.
18 N. Abercrombie *et al.*, *The Dominant Ideology Thesis*, London, 1980.
19 *ODM*, 11–12.

20 ibid., 200.
21 *EL*, 10–11.
22 ibid., 25.
23 ibid., 57.
24 A. MacIntyre, op. cit., 90.
25 *EL*, 26.
26 I owe this second definition of tolerance to Albert Weale.
27 *EL*, 62, 79.
28 T. Potter, 'The end of terror', *Socialist Review*, 51, February 1983.
29 *EL*, 60.
30 Marx and Engels, *Collected Works* (50 vols published or in preparation, London, 1975–), V. 4.
31 A. MacIntyre, op. cit., 22.
32 *ODM*, 192.
33 I have discussed Marx's conception of proletarian self-emancipation at some length in my *The Revolutionary Ideas of Karl Marx*, London, 1983.
34 L. Trotsky, *The Struggle against Fascism in Germany*, New York, 1970, 155–6. See also N. Poulantzas, *Fascisme et dictature*, Paris, 1970; C. Sparks, 'Fascism and the working class', *International Socialism*, 2:2 (1978) and 2:3 (1978/9); and C. Sparks, *Never Again!*, London, 1980.
35 ibid., 30–1.
36 J. S. Mill, *On Liberty*, ed. G. Himmelfarb, Harmondsworth, 1974, 119.
37 The significance of this underlying shift became clear only during the original discussion of this paper. I remember especially the points raised by David Edwards and Susan Mendus.
38 M. Walker, *The National Front*, London, 1977.
39 C. Ricks, 'Dark Tom', *London Review of Books*, 5: 22/3, 1–21 December 1983. I am aware that I have left without discussion such important questions as the manner in which a prohibition of fascist groups might be enforced, but this raises much larger issues (centring upon the nature of the contemporary Western state) which it would be foolish to touch on in an essay of this length.

4

Toleration and the English blasphemy law

DAVID EDWARDS

Blasphemy has been held to be the greatest of sins, and in the period when sin and crime were hardly distinguished, it was thought to be the greatest of crimes. In England during the years from 1400 to 1612, death by fire was the penalty for the worst cases of blasphemy. The accommodation of what was thought to be blasphemous was the furthest stretch of religious toleration. When England made its first experiments with religious toleration in the Commonwealth period, the trial of Naylor (1656), who had been worshipped as 'the lamb of God', was its severest test, and the fact that he escaped with his life (though little else) its greatest triumph.[1] In the 1977 *Gay News* blasphemy case, to some it seemed incredible that in this day and age a person could be in danger of a jail sentence for offending against religious sensitivities, but for others the question at issue was 'Is nothing sacred?'

Blasphemy as a criminal offence was originally subject to the jurisdiction of the medieval Church courts.[2] This was a highly miscellaneous and extensive jurisdiction, but its chief feature was that the whole population was answerable to it in respect of immoral conduct and heterodox opinion. The 'Courts Christian' had the duty of repressing sin, and such misconduct as drunkenness, adultery, fornication, procuring, homosexual offences and abortion were considered to be violations of Christianity understood as a moral code. These courts were also charged with the repression of offences against the Christianity composed by the orthodox dogmas of the Church. The punishment of blasphemy as a crime was integral to this jurisdiction. The Church courts survived the Reformation, though they subsequently derived their authority from the Crown and the orthodoxy which they enforced was greatly modified. From Elizabeth's time the ecclesiastical courts were subject to the Court of High Commission, which, by the Act which constituted it, was obliged not to treat as crimes of heresy those points at issue between Protestant and Catholic. This jurisdiction was made impotent in 1640, when the Court of High Commission and the sanctions of the subordinate ecclesiastical courts were abolished.

The offence of blasphemy at common law effectively dates from Taylor's case in 1676, when the court of King's Bench took cognizance of the crime inherited from the defunct jurisdiction. Taylor was a madman who was lodged in Bedlam prior to his trial. His offence was that he denounced Christ as a bastard and whore-master and religion as a cheat, along with making various crazy claims about himself. These circumstances are bizarre but insignificant compared with the fact that the case was considered to merit the attention of the Lord Chief Justice and formed the precedent for a major extension of common law jurisdiction. The Chief Justice, Sir Matthew Hale, observed that Taylor's

> wicked and blasphemous words were not only an offence against God and religion, but a crime against the laws, State and Government, and therefore punishable in this Court; that to say religion is a cheat is to dissolve all those obligations whereby civil societies are preserved; and Christianity being parcel of the laws of England, therefore to reproach the Christian religion is to speak in subversion of the law.[3]

Christianity is to be protected as the basis of civil obligation and the sanction of law; blasphemy is to be punished as a species of subversion. Hale's dictum long continued to be cited as authoritative in blasphemy trials. Its spirit seems to be that all fundamental attacks on Christianity are criminal offences, no matter how pure the misguided motive of the offender or discreet the language employed. An Act of William III (there were never any prosecutions under this Act, but it was a major buttress of the common law offence) treats the simple denial of Christianity as a crime. However, the judges, though they often acted harshly in particular cases of blasphemy, seem to have been daunted by the simple rigour of the law construed in this way. Gradually, the doctrine crept into the law that the manner, not the matter, of the utterance constituted the crime of blasphemy. It did not entirely supplant the seventeenth-century view, so the character of the law became ambiguous. Did the law forbid all public denials of the truth of Christianity, or only offensively expressed attacks on the Christian religion? If the latter was the principle on which courts acted, was this a recognition of a legal right to decorous free speech on religious matters or a prudent concession by the authorities which implied no such right? Was the *raison d'être* of the law Hale's view that the sanctions of Christianity were essential to the integrity of the law, or was its purpose the protection of the feelings of the pious from insult? The resolution of these ambiguities was the task of the legislature and the judiciary, but Parliament was (and still is) very reluctant to resolve such charged matters, and, prior to 1883, the practices of the courts continued to be equivocal. The decisive influence in forcing change, not surprisingly, was public opinion.

For all the strength of the spontaneous forces of social inhibition present in Victorian England, there was also an increasing suspicion of the regulation of free discussion by the public authorities. Even where the majority approved the punishment of convicted blasphemers, this was regarded as a justifiable departure from a supposed right to free discussion of religious matters. I say 'supposed right', because on a strict construction of the common law of blasphemy and the statute of William III no such right existed. But the popular view was that England was a free country, and the judges, infected by this prejudice, had suffered the law to become ambiguous in order to accommodate such a view. But the accommodation had to become consistent, and it only finally did so in 1883 with the trial of Foote and Ramsey for blasphemous libel. (Foote and Ramsey were respectively editor and publisher of the magazine *Freethinker*, the 1882 Christmas issue of which was filled with festively anti-religious cartoons and doggerels.) The judge, Lord Chief Justice Coleridge, ruled in that case that 'if the decencies of controversy are observed, even the fundamentals of religion may be attacked without the writer being guilty of blasphemy'. This marks a stage in the history of the blasphemy law, resolving the former ambiguity in favour of the distinction between matter and manner. Although Coleridge's dictum was controversial, it became authoritative. Coleridge's most distinguished critic was Sir J. F. Stephen, who argued that the Chief Justice's ruling was an unsound interpretation of the law, and that as the blasphemy law was fundamentally bad, it should be annulled by Parliament. Since (despite initial dissent from the judicial bench) Coleridge's interpretation of the law was made the basis of subsequent judge's rulings, even such critics as Stephen were eventually compelled to accept its authoritative status.

Notwithstanding Parliamentary attempts at annulment in the 1880s, 1930s and 1970s, blasphemy remains a crime in common law. Lord Scarman's judgment (given in the 1977 *Gay News* case) is that Stephen's *Digest of the Criminal Law* (following Coleridge) gives a correct formula of the modern law:

> Every publication is said to be blasphemous which contains any contemptuous, reviling, scurrilous or ludicrous matter relating to God, Jesus Christ, or the Bible, or the formulas of the Church of England as by law established. It is not blasphemous to speak or publish opinions hostile to the Christian religion, or to deny the existence of God, if the publication is couched in decent and temperate language. The test to be applied is as to the manner in which the doctrines are advocated and not as to the substance of the doctrines themselves.[4]

This formula governed a series of late Victorian and early twentieth-century trials for blasphemy the last of which ended in the conviction of J. W. Gott in 1922. Since that time there have been only two events of major significance regarding this offence, and both involve obscenity rather than failure to observe the decencies of controversy. In 1976, a Danish film-maker, Jens Jorgen Thorsen, proposed to make a pornographic film of a fantasized sex life of Jesus, bringing out the implications of Jesus' manhood in the context of supposed male and female lovers. Thorsen intended to make the film in Britain, until a chorus of protest induced him to desist. The Prime Minister and the Archbishop of Canterbury referred to the possibility of a prosecution under the common law of blasphemy: the Queen let it be known that she viewed the project as 'obnoxious'. Shortly afterwards

Mary Whitehouse undertook a private prosecution against *Gay News*, the homosexual newspaper, and its editor, Denis Lemon. They had published a poem by James Kirkup which involved a fantasy of homosexual intercourse with the crucified corpse of Jesus and imputed to him promiscuous homosexual encounters, with partners singly and in groups. The author evidently regarded his work as an act of pious meditation and the editor professed to have published with the motive of offering spiritual consolation and accommodation to his readers. The *Gay News* trial took place at the London Central Criminal Court before Mr Justice King-Hamilton, himself a Jew but a 'sympathiser with Christianity'. He ruled that, despite the lapse of over half a century since the last prosecution, blasphemy remained a crime at common law; the statute of William III had finally been repealed in 1967, but the common law offence, being left intact, was (if anything) affirmed. He further ruled that tendency to provoke a breach of the peace was a relevant consideration for the jury and that the essential question in the case was whether the publication was blasphemous, and not whether it was the intention of the accused to blaspheme. After Lemon's conviction, the judge sentenced him to nine months' imprisonment, suspended for eighteen months; fined him £500 and regarded this punishment as inclining to leniency.

The Thorsen episode and *Gay News* case not surprisingly gave rise to a Speakers' Corner hubbub of confused debate and declamation. Contributions came from palaces royal and episcopal, from anarchist pamphleteers, the House of Lords, the organized ranks of the National Secular Society and the Festival of Light, and from individual writers of letters to the newspapers. Lord Willis followed the previous attempts to have the common law offence abolished, arguing that laws on obscenity, indecency and conduct likely to cause a breach of the peace were adequate safeguards for decency and order. His proposal was over-whelmingly defeated in the House of Lords. The Law Commission produced a working paper proposing that in place of the offence of blasphemy there be a new offence of using threatening, insulting or abusive words or behaviour in a place of worship. In response to this, the Archbishop of Canterbury (Dr Runcie) suggested that the law of blasphemy not only be retained but be extended to religions other than Christianity 'with the object of protecting the fundamental, sacred beliefs of all religious people from deep and hurtful attack', though acknowledging the difficulty of defining those religions which should receive legal protection.[5]

The *Gay News* conviction was appealed to the Court of Appeal and to the House of Lords, being dismissed on both occasions. Of the five judgments in the House of Lords, two would have allowed the appeal on the ground that proof of intention to blaspheme should be brought home to defendants. None of the Law Lords believed that the offence of blasphemy was a dead letter, and Lord Scarman advanced the view that the scope of the offence should be extended by new legislation. In his judgment he says:

> The offence belongs to a group of criminal offences designed to safeguard the internal tranquillity of the Kingdom. In an increasingly plural society such as that of modern Britain, it is necessary not only to respect the differing religious beliefs, feelings and practices of all but also to protect them from scurrility, vilification and contempt. . . . It would be intolerable if, by allowing an author or publisher to plead the excellence of his motives and the right of free speech, he could evade the penalties of the law, even though his words were blasphemous in the sense of constituting an outrage upon the religious feelings of his fellow citizens. This is no way forward for a successful plural society.

★

The present common law of blasphemy assumed its character as a result of adaptation to some of the beliefs and values that prevailed in the last century. We have seen that this was a painful and ambiguous process of adaptation that resulted in the establishment of the present legal criterion. The law, as it currently stands, prohibits the expression of contempt, scurrility and ridicule towards what is taken to be the core of the Christian religion and it has been proposed that such protection be extended to other, or all, religions. The purpose of the law is to protect believers, and sympathizers with religious belief, from mortification and offence.[6] Such offence may be provoked as a result of a deliberate attack on religious beliefs, or by perceived perversion and abuse of those beliefs even where no attack is intended. The exhibition of opinions hostile or offensive to religious belief is, of course, allowed by the law, but gross intemperance and indecency are not. It may be thought that the law is, therefore, permissive towards the substance of all opinions and expressions on religious affairs, merely prohibiting avoidably (and so gratuitously) offensive forms of expression. But some thoughts, if expressed, are inherently reviling, contemptuous and insulting of religious belief and there are modes of expression where the form and substance of thought cannot be divorced (such as poems and pictures). Here it cannot be said that the offence is gratuitous, but it is none the less illegal.

The term 'offence' covers a multitude of reactions, from mild annoyance to explosive outrage or profound heartache, and it is only fair to infer that the purpose of the present law, or any proposed extended law, is to deter and punish those publications which provoke the most severe forms of distress. Again, in considering the merits of any extension of the law of blasphemy I suppose that the general character of the existing law will not be transformed and in particular that most substantive attacks and violations of religious belief will be allowable, but that the law will enforce 'decency of manner'.

I propose to discuss the nature and propriety of the current law of blasphemy and of any future extension of his law, and so will begin by outlining two arguments, one of which denies and the other affirms the fitness of such a law. The issue is a radical one (going to the root of many current beliefs) and provokes an examination of many different questions of jurisprudence, politics, ethics and religion, and I intend only to touch on some of these. All kinds of points of view might be advanced on such a matter, but I feel it most profitable to restrict attention to a consideration of the most conservative – that is, those which are most plausible in the light of prevailing beliefs and dispositions and which venture least beyond persuading us to a desired conclusion on the issue. Anarchists, would-be Grand Inquisitors and militant devil-worshippers have relevant views, but I have left them out of account.

An argument against the propriety of the blasphemy law might be made on the following lines. The society we have come to be is marked by the same diversity of enthusiasm and indifference in regard to religion as it is in everything else. In our current circumstances, spiritual life, like sport or politics, offers its own possibilities for passion, imaginative adventure and apathy. The claims of prophets and hierarchies, of preachers and enlighteners are all candidates before the bar of individual judgement. Whatever the claims made for any gospel such a judgement alone is competent to acknowledge or reject. All authority ascribed to religious beliefs, scriptures, rites and officials derives from the same act of personal choice. No coercion constrains the authority of individual conviction; between individuals nothing is immune from criticism. The determination of spiritual value is a matter of persuasion, of exposition, and (perhaps) argument, and in any such process there must be the possibility of contradiction, condemnation and offence. Choice and liberty would seem to apply to religious affairs quite as much as to hairstyles or home decoration. Choice and liberty give rise to variety, and for the items that make up this variety, we may feel incomprehension or admiration, indifference, tolerance or disgust. In our present surroundings, controversy and censure are not to be avoided – such fields as those of sexual conduct and political partisanship are inseparable from anger, loathing and disdain. And when, in the sphere of religion, we see the same variety, the same controversy and strength of feeling, we must expect to see the same contradiction, often angry and intemperate; the same exaggerations and vehemence and expressions of ridicule and contempt.

Such offence and rough contention, it will be said, is regrettable but inseparable from the extension of a regime of freedom beyond the realms of trivia to those issues where strong feelings are involved. Where the choice is between monopoly and privilege on the one hand and hurt and antagonism on the other, the free society must opt for contention. Of course, there are limits to antagonism, mainly voluntary restraints on giving offence, though some are necessarily coercions by the use of law: violence to persons, property and reputation is forbidden and must be repressed. Such restraints apply to propaganda and dispute concerning moral practices and political affairs, and, of course, must apply to matters of spiritual controversy. But why should any further restraints be applied to those forms of expression involved in religious affairs? In religious no more than in political persuasion, is there any orthodoxy which everyone spontaneously acknowledges or is imposed by authority? No conformity of belief is required, nor should it be. Nothing in religious belief is unassailable; all claims are open to scrutiny and rejection. This must equally apply to any claim to particular deference in the treatment of religious subjects. There may be good grounds for granting special circumspection in this area, or there may be none. But the sole arbiter of this question should be the judgement of individuals; they have the right to assent to or dissent from religious belief and acknowledge or repudiate religious authority and, therefore, theirs is the right to judge the related claim of religions of entitlement to special restraint and avoidance of giving offence. No religious belief has any coercive authority beyond what it can induce by persuasion, and this limitation should also apply to any claim it advances about the deference in manner due to it by dissentients, competitors or opponents. This applies to any one system of religious beliefs and to any collection of such systems; the number of adherents involved is not a relevant matter. Particular religions and the whole set of religions are candidates claiming recognition of value, and the competence for deciding their claims is vested with the individual. Similarly, when a particular religion or set of religions makes a claim to special restraint or scrupulous treatment from those who are disposed to attack or dissent from them, there also the competence for deciding that claim should lie with the individual concerned. A law of blasphemy enforcing with penal sanctions special forms of restraint and inhibition in the treatment of religious matters is an anomaly having no place in our social arrangements.

So much for an argument against the blasphemy law; what kind of reply might be made in its favour? It might be objected that, although there is much to be said for the preceding view of our circumstances, such an account leaves too much out of the reckoning and, in particular, gives a distorted account of the claims of religion. Considerations that might be decisive in terms of trade or preference do not apply there; the elements that turn the scale in favour of some circumstantial protection of religious belief have

been given short weight. It is true that there is no external compulsion to religious belief or observance in our society, and in that
restricted sense, religion is a matter of 'choice'. But the notion of
a 'choice of religion' in any more extended sense is a profane
illusion. If a religious belief *is* a religious belief, the believer has no
choice in the matter; the believer simply acknowledges what is, for
him, an undeniable reality. That process by which religious belief
is evoked is indeed voluntary, and to that extent is a process of
persuasion, but it is also coercive – a person is not 'persuaded' to
exercise a choice in the manner in which a consumer is wooed by
an advertiser, but rather is compelled to a recognition of a new
reality. The term which we use to denote such a process is
'conversion'; it is not only compulsory for the believer but is a
transformation of the self; the religious believer not only has no
choice but to believe, but is a different person in the light of that
belief.

Moreover, it might be maintained, to hold a religious belief is
different in degree and type from other 'opinions'. The recognition of what is 'sacred' involves an affirmation of what is believed
to be of ultimate value in experience, and of what is of deepest
concern in life. In a profession of religious faith a person states the
most powerful conviction that it is possible to make; to the believer
it is absolute and unqualified. These characteristics of religious
belief – that it is ultimate and compelling – are the reasons why
rights to religious freedom are accorded special status in national
constitutions and international declarations of rights. The extra-
ordinary power and scope of religious concern is rightly recognized as the ground of a special entitlement of the believer, and (it
is maintained) it follows by implication that this 'imposes a duty
on all of us to refrain from insulting or outraging the religious
feelings of others' (Lord Scarman). Other people have a prima-
facie claim to civil treatment from us, perhaps even our respect,
and this claim is greatly intensified when we are dealing with their
religious beliefs. In religion, people's beliefs are convictions that
they are compelled to, they are the most solemn and absolute that
can be held, and the feelings of the believer are at their most
vulnerable. Consequently, the right of the believer to be protected
from outrage is of a different order from that prevailing in other
spheres, and if the restraint and decency of treatment are not

accorded voluntarily, then the law must interpose to offer protection.

This reply grounds the case for the protection of religious beliefs from outrage in those features of such beliefs that are claimed to be specific and unique. It avoids ascribing 'truth' to any particular religion, or invoking such controversial doctrines as that which endows majorities with the right to use the criminal law to enforce their strongest disapprovals or that which maintains that religious belief is entitled to special protection because it is an essential ancillary to good conduct.

In terms of their acceptability to current moral beliefs, these two arguments seem to me to be the most plausible and cautious case for a decision for or against the existence of a blasphemy law. The matter at issue between them, of course, is the balance to be struck between the supposed rights to 'free expression' and to be protected against outrage. Attending to the previous arguments, we see that neither side need give no weight to the considerations that the other takes as decisive. A case against the blasphemy laws can concede that provoking an outrage can be a candidate element for legal punishment, and a case for the blasphemy laws may agree that free expression is usually of the greatest value. We need not abandon a readiness to punish slander, incitement to riot or sexual exhibitionism to assert that religious sensitivities should be given no special protection by the law; we need not espouse the view that any and all offensive expression merits penal sanctions to take the view that gross outrages on religious belief should be punishable.

Let us examine more closely the implications of punishing blasphemy because of the offence caused to believers. In grounding the law of blasphemy on a sole concern to protect religious believers and sympathizers from being offended, the law may be said to have become both less restrictive and less liberal. The satisfaction of injured feelings has no doubt always been an element in the law, but the older stages of the law took into account further harm supposed to have been inflicted by blasphemous utterances. Incurring divine retribution, imperilling an enforced orthodoxy essential to the salvation of the faithful, subverting the conditions of civil association and the sanction of the system of law – all these (if true) are powerful claims against the exercise of liberty, which even those who value it most highly must take into account. But should outrage and wounded feelings ever be the sole ground for a law, or should such elements only be taken into account as an aggravation of injuries which are punished because of some further harm inflicted?[7]

I find any absolute distinction between offence and harm impossible to sustain, if the category of 'offence' is extended to those shocks which can cause long-lasting or permanent disorientations or impairments. Intense shame, guilt, anger and mortification can be provoked by 'offence' and can, it is claimed, cast a lasting shadow over life. Indeed, even without taking duration into the reckoning, any sharp wound to the feelings is, to that extent, an injury (though the harm involved is often more than compensated by consequent benefits). For these reasons I cannot agree with those who maintain that the punishment and prevention of offence can never (on principle) be the substantive ground for a legal prohibition. But this is an extremely reluctant admission, for the danger of any extended use of legal coercion on grounds of offence will be apparent to anyone who remotely cares for liberty. Without going into other reasons for the most cautious use of the notion of offence in the criminal law, let me note that much keen offence is inevitable if human society is to be distinguished from an ant-hill, and, more to the point, that much offence is beneficial, and is inseparable from the vitality of thought and spirit.

If the criminal law is to be invoked to offer protection against violation of beliefs, then those beliefs must be regarded as worthy of respect, if not admiration. There is, of course, the alternative motive of simply keeping peace and quiet, but I do not think this is the decisive motive for advocates of a blasphemy law. It could well be that the punishment of blasphemy provokes more controversy than it quells. Any advocacy of a law of blasphemy must, surely, assume that the protected belief is worthy of respect, and that the violation of a minimum show of respect should be punished, if necessary, by use of penal sanctions (any increase in peace and quiet being a bonus).[8]

What kinds of belief are worthy of respect, and so entitled to minimum deference that specific criminal laws should protect them from indecent treatment? The answer to this is surely not that respect-worthiness applies to all beliefs of which someone asserts that they are his religious beliefs. 'Respect' in the relevant sense means that we esteem a person or belief; we recognize a value in them, even if we do not agree with them. Esteem has to be merited; promiscuous, indiscriminate 'respect' is not a sign of generous sympathy but of moral chaos. It is true (and, I think, the opening for confusion) that we also use the term 'respect' for certain forbearances where no attribution of merit is implied; we might 'respect the right of someone to go his own way', even if we thought the particular preference utterly worthless. Any deference, in this case, is to the 'right'; 'respect' refers to the right, and not to the selection. This sense of respect (of forbearance, avoiding interference with) is, of course, shown in the history and practice of religious toleration. All religious beliefs (not involving criminal conduct) might be respected in the meagrest sense of 'tolerated', but this will hardly yield the conclusion that they are, therefore, entitled to esteem and to a legally enforced minimum deference.

If the law of blasphemy is to be extended this question of appraisal (Is a given religion worthy of esteem?) is of great practical moment. As we have seen, in the evolution of the law of blas-phemy, the value of Christianity was axiomatic. It was the very heart of the ecclesiastical jurisdiction, and 'parcel' of the common law jurisdiction that adopted the punishment of the crime of blasphemy. Since 1883, the reasons for a circumstantial legal pro-tection of Christianity, and it alone, have not been clear, but might be defended on mutually reinforcing grounds: that a majority of the population believed it to be true; that a greater majority of the population as 'sympathizers' believed it to merit a circumstantial legal protection; that although law-abidingness might not absolutely depend on Christian beliefs, these were still the origin of many legally enforced practices (monogamy, etc.) and were a valuable ancillary to civil association worth protecting from gross insult. Whatever the merits of such a case might be, it is not one which can be transferred wholesale to any other religion, let alone all religions.

That religious belief, *per se*, is not entitled to respect, let alone veneration, will be evident to anyone with a cursory knowledge of human history. There is probably no abomination known to man that has not, at some time and place, been part of some religious worship, if not the very object of religious worship. In

87

the view of some atheists, all religious belief is inherently degrading and corrupting, and the reasons they advance are not
manifestly fatuous or to be rejected out of hand. However this may
be, in England today there is no consensus of respect for the
religious beliefs of the Rastafarians, the Scientologists, the
Unification Church, Voodooists and Satanists. There are, if we
can believe the newspapers, cults which incorporate practices of
drug abuse and sex with children as part of a religious discipline;
there are others which seem to be for the enrichment of confidence
tricksters or the gratification of small-time power maniacs. The
Guardian (unfairly) said of Dr Runcie's proposals, 'Animists would
thus be included [in legal protection] so that it would be an offence
to speak mockingly of anything which animists venerate, and since
some polytheists see God in everything it would be an offence to
speak mockingly at all.'[9] This is unfair, because it is admitted by
the proponents of extended legal protection that distinctions must
be made between claimant religious beliefs. But this distinction can
hardly be on the ground that those not selected for circumstantial
protection from offence are not religions, or not authentic
religions. It is sheer self-deceit and a misrepresentation of mankind's past and present to pretend that objects of detestation to
some have not been objects of worship (and authentic worship) to
others. (Professor Kirkup's poem in *Gay News* was judged by the
court to be blasphemous, but this does not necessarily invalidate
its claim to be a 'religious' composition, although it does imply
that it was not worthy of legal protection.) The distinction must
be based on 'respect-worthiness' rather than authenticity as
religion.

This implication of any extension of the blasphemy law must
give pause for thought. I cannot see how any such revision of the
law could do other than extend a legal recognition of 'respect-
worthiness' to a list of approved religions by Act of Parliament or
the setting-up of a criterion to the same effect. The difficulties of
establishing a criterion will appal all but the most intrepid, but
even if this is surmounted, what of the result? It is true that diverse
religions (though not Christianity) achieved a protected status in
Imperial Rome and that a plurality of religions have this status in
other countries today. In the days of the British Empire, an Order
in Council was issued in 1904 which sought to restrain over-

zealous missionaries by forbidding to British subjects any public derision or insult directed against religions observed in China or Korea made while resident within those countries. For all that, the idea of legally 'respect-worthy religions' seems to me to be more out of keeping with our present society than its opponents might claim of the present surviving circumstantial protection of what once was (and notionally still is) the national religion. The making of such judgments of value as I believe are implied in extending the blasphemy law seems to be a disquieting modification of the office of our legislature, whatever the exigencies of 'a successful plural society'.

To recapitulate, the mere fact of offence caused by 'indecent treatment' of some religion does not justify the extension to it of legal protection. If the sanctions of the criminal law are to be invoked, the religious belief must be regarded as worthy of respect (in the sense of being estimable), even if not believed in. For the non-believer, the question is not 'If I believed in that, shouldn't I want it to receive legal protection?' but rather, 'Given that I don't believe that, do I none the less perceive in the belief sufficient value to justify punishment of those who grossly offend the people who do believe it?' And, it goes without saying that, as in all considered enactments of criminal law, the question is not 'Do I believe that offering gross insults to other people's religious beliefs is right or wrong?' but rather, 'Should we send people to jail for it?'

Let us examine more closely the implications of the law of blasphemy for freedom of expression. This is a vague term, and although people sometimes speak as if freedom of expression should be absolutely unqualified, a moment's thought would remind them that there are many areas of speech and conduct where expression is rightly restricted, of which the hackneyed example that no one has the right to (lyingly) yell 'Fire!' in a crowded theatre recalls only one. What may be represented as a more plausible unqualified right is the right to advance opinions, regardless of the offence caused. Indeed, the case for free expression of opinion incorporates the proposition that, not only is offence not to be avoided, but that it is actually beneficial. We could be lukewarm in our opinions if indignation did not spur us to their defence; we come to believe more deeply and vividly when our views are under assault; the shock of having them demolished converts us to a contrary opinion. The whole vocabulary of the theoretical grounds of free debate is shot through with terms of antagonism and offence; the presiding notion is that of 'argument'.[10]

Where religious sensitivities are affronted by opinion and argument, there can never be a case for legal prohibition. The offended have means of redress ready to their hand in resources of counter-argument. The law of blasphemy became reconciled to this in 1883, but adapted to enforce 'decency of manner'. When heresy was seen as a species of blasphemy most instances of the crime consisted in the denial of propositions and formulae extracted from creeds and theological doctrines. The criminal law was indeed used in those cases as a substitute for argument. Argument provides its own devices of offence and defence; if not stringent procedures of evidence and proof, at least forms of dissent and contradiction going beyond mere assertion and denial in an effort to persuade (persuade at least ourselves). Scientific and historical controversies have shocked religious feelings, yet not only do those disciplines provide weapons for counter-attack, but also the controversies themselves have deepened and enriched religious belief and thought.

Take the case of what Albert Schweitzer has termed 'the quest for the historical Jesus'. The historical investigation of the life of Jesus was a triumph of nineteenth-century German scholarship: before Coleridge's interpretation of the common law of blasphemy became authoritative (Stephen believed) its most important products should have run the risk of prosecution in England. This enquiry was brought before an English public through the agency of Renan's derivative work, and the resulting wave of thought is an important factor in the development of the blasphemy law. Schweitzer says of the investigation that it was 'the most tremendous thing which the religious consciousness has ever dared and done'. It called on all the resources of the investigators' spirit as well as intellect: Schweitzer states:

> There is no historical task which so reveals a man's true self as the writing of a life of Jesus. . . . No vital force comes into the figure unless a man breathes into it all the hate or all the love of which he is capable. . . . For hate as well as love can write a

life of Jesus, and the greatest of them are written with hate.[11]

In considering historical hypotheses attributing to Jesus such characteristics as fraud, ambition, fanaticism and duplicity, the historical insight of the investigators motivated by hate was greatly sharpened. In Schweitzer's view this minority advanced the study of the subject more than all the others put together: 'But for the offence which they caused, the science of historical theology would not have stood where it does today.'

On Schweitzer's account, hatred, cruelty, renunciation and the deepest offence were necessary not only to open a field to historical investigation, but also to prevent religious thought from being fossilized. What has this to do with the blasphemy law's concern, which is not to proscribe offensive opinions, but to deter indecency of manner? Partly this illustration again reminds us that the substance of an opinion is generally more wounding than its expression, but more importantly it demonstrates that antagonism is essential to the vitality of mind and spirit. Experiences of ridicule, contempt, scorn, vilification are an integral part of serious argument. Whether they are deserved or properly employed depends on the merits of the tenor of the argument itself, which the law avowedly does not judge. The remedy for those offended lies not in suppression of an opinion or circumlocution of expression, but the use of counter-argument. In the current law of blasphemy, 'the test to be applied is as to the manner in which the doctrines are advocated and not as to the substance of the doctrines themselves' (Stephen's *Digest*).[12] I believe that, even though the test is intended to be of form rather than of substance, it is still an impairment of those conditions of argument that are a spring of mental energy. As long as argument is possible, the affronted parties can return in kind, or have the greater satisfaction of believing themselves to have carried the contested point.

Religious advocacy in particular shows a degree of antagonism and vehemence that has never been exceeded. To the partisans, their 'opinion' was often a matter of more than life and death importance; they were doing battle with the very root of all evils; the issue concerned no small audience but the whole human race. As Stephen asks,

Was any form of Christianity ever substituted either for

paganism or any other form of Christianity without heat, exaggeration and fierce invective? . . . How can you expect men to discuss such questions as the doctrine of the atonement or the doctrine of eternal punishment as calmly as they might discuss questions of philology?

The passionate propagation of religion (or the denial of one) inevitably involves offence:

All the more earnest and enthusiastic forms of religion are extremely offensive to those who do not believe them. Why should not people who are not Christians be protected against the rough, coarse, ignorant ferocity with which they are often told that they and theirs are on the way to hell-fire for ever and ever? Such a doctrine, though necessary to be known if true, is, if false, revolting and mischievous to the last degree.[13]

In disputes concerning religion, then, the stakes are so high and the interested parties so passionate and numerous that circumstantial restraints (of decency, deference) amount to a prohibition of authentic expression of opinion.

However, not all 'expression' is the venturing of an opinion, and not all expression offers purchase for an argument; we may be outraged by it, but we cannot 'get to grips with it'. This is the case, for example, with pictures and poems (unless they are versified arguments and bad poems). Here, any offence caused gives no opportunity for combat and redress. Outrage is powerless because perforce speechless; it is struck dumb, not by the enormity of an opinion or the indecency of its expression, but because the source of offence is impervious to denial, let alone refutation. This, it seems to me, is the more important distinction between Professor Kirkup's poem and Bishop Montefiore's suggestion that Jesus may have been a homosexual. The crucial distinction is not that Kirkup was obscene while Montefiore was highly circumspect, but that the latter advanced an argument (a sketch of a historical hypothesis with associated theological interpretation) while the former, who merely presented an image, left his objectors in impotent fury.

Although the current blasphemy law prohibits indecency in arguments against the Christian religion, it may be doubted whether any successful prosecution could now be brought fitting this description. We may infer from the Thorsen and *Gay News* affairs that what the law currently protects is neither the doctrines of the Christian religion nor its claim to decency of treatment in argument, but rather its 'images of piety'. I mean by this expression those symbolic conceptions of piety and holiness such as a rite, a Calvary or a pietà. What the law is punishing is not heterodoxy or indecent vehemence in argument, but rather a public performance of iconoclasm.

A word about religion, no matter how brief or clumsy, is perhaps appropriate when discussing the blasphemy law. It seems to me that these religious symbols, images of piety, can be distinguished as belonging to two orders, though the actual symbols used to represent them tend to combine the two aspects. One order of religious images expresses a relation of sympathy and identification between believer and image; they evoke in the believer such emotions as comfort, pride, consolation and grateful affection. They represent the form of religion which Matthew Arnold styles 'morality tinged with emotion', which can range in depth from a profoundly considered devotion, to that where God is placed alongside the household deities of Mother and Apple Pie. This piety and its images is part of being at home in the world; it can command the most intense loyalty, and the violation of its images can provoke the deepest offence. None the less, I think that such images are of the same kind as other non-religious symbols of loyalty and veneration that come to mind when we think of objects whose violation causes 'offence'. These secular images which may be 'desecrated' – flags (in flag-burnings), war memorials, images of childhood (in erotic contexts), images of the Royal family, Karl Marx's tomb – do not belong to a different order.

The other order of religious imagery is not at all representative of a relation of sympathy and identification, but is rather an attempt to intimate the reality of 'another world', utterly different from the one we know, anything that it could become or, indeed, anything which we can clearly conceive. Far from being a contribution to being 'at home in the world', this experience of God is one of radical 'otherness', at which human analogies of majesty, wrath or glory can only hint. This mysterious experience (which Rudolf Otto termed 'the numinous')[14] is essentially uncanny, overpowering and awful, but is to be understood in a manner categorically different from those events explained in a quasi-scientific manner as 'supernatural' or 'miraculous'. Such an encounter may bring bliss or the peril of annihilation, but re-assurance or accommodation is to be sought elsewhere; it not only disturbs our equanimity, but qualifies our very sense of self as an identity which is essentially or perfectly real.

A conception of 'the holy' belongs to both orders of religious imagery, but I think that the context of the idea of blasphemy is to be found in that encounter with a transcendent reality that is the 'numinous'. The offence which is given to the believer is horror at the violation of the symbols and images which, at least as ideograms, point to the sacred mystery. (Inappropriate imagery is itself such a violation; Judaism and Islam have images of speech and symbol to express the numinous, but use of the plastic arts is a desecration because blasphemously inappropriate.) The idea of 'the holy' can be a great intensification of those values (goodness, purity, mercy, wisdom) that are not only precious, but familiar; but the authentic root of 'blasphemy' is surely desecration of the 'holiness' of which our secular experience provides only the germ of an analogy.

The numinous is not to be thought of, or talked about, says Tillich, without the embarrassments of tact, doubt and awe.[15] The idea of 'protecting' it is not so much irreverent as fatuous. Certain images expressing the numinous may be protected ('15 military policemen were called out ... yesterday ... to restore order at Stonehenge where fireworks and an unruly mob threatened to prevent the Druids from carrying out their annual summer solstice ceremonies').[16] Certainly the law can undertake to deter and punish violations of such images, out of consideration for the offence caused to believers.

The inevitable reserve attached to the idea of 'the holy', and the absurdity of 'protecting' it; its resistance to being assimilated to other 'interests' that the law might defend or advance gives to the history of the blasphemy laws a curious air of unreality – 'Hamlet without the Prince'. 'Blasphemy' in terms of the law seems to undergo a process of displacement, like that which a straight stick appears to suffer when partly immersed in water. I have throughout used the notions of 'Christianity' which have been complementary to the various stages of the blasphemy law. But the 'Christianity' which is the true context of blasphemy is always to one side of those understandings in which it denotes a theological orthodoxy or code of proper conduct; a sanction of civil obligation or origination of various legal prohibitions; a general susceptibility to be disputed with circumstantial decency.

The numinous, or those intensifications of moral and aesthetic experience that are 'holy' cannot be 'desecrated' or 'protected' (any more than sunbeams can be protected or defiled); the reverse is true of the images which express them. Should the law seek to punish such desecrations? The same considerations of vitality of thought and propaganda that can be advanced against legal control not only of opinion and argument about religion, but vehement and passionate argument, would seem to extend to such symbolic iconoclasm. Against these considerations there may be urged various differences between the invective of argument and such iconoclasm (in terms of greater offensiveness, the dubious claim that iconoclasm is needlessly 'gratuitous', or that nothing can be learned from such 'expression'), but the chief difference, I think, is in terms of what response can be made in each case. The most vituperative argument against Christianity offers a resource of counter-argument in a way in which the most mildly pornographic film of the supposed sex life of Jesus does not.

When outrage is necessarily speechless, violence is near. In a world where beauty contests and animal experiments occasion acts of violence, the view that Kirkup's poem or Thorsen's proposed film are unlikely to have provoked such consequences is a very rosy one. This is not to claim, of course, that any propensity to violence is in itself a claim to call in the law as surrogate avenger, or to depreciate the virtue of resisting anger despite provocation. But where those offended are judged to have good cause to be profoundly wounded and distressed by desecrations that are in no way arguments and left with no means of rejoinder short of violence, I do not see why (as a matter of principle) the law should not interpose on their behalf. Whether this requires a specific law of blasphemy is a technical question for legislators and their legal advisers. For my own part I should greatly prefer that it did not. To have a blasphemy law (or 'Offences against Religious Feelings Act') invites all manner of irrelevant criticism and mis-

95

representation (for instance, that it is disposed of by quoting the Emperor Tiberius to the effect that 'wrongs done to the gods are the gods' concern', as though this had ever had anything to do with the common law). To retain the blasphemy law probably (and rightly) means extending its protection to religions other than Christianity, but not to all – an invidious and unsavoury proceeding. The present law is certainly unduly restrictive, in prohibiting even 'indecency' in argument; my own view would be that punishable 'blasphemy' should both be obscene (to do with sex and excretion) and have no place in argument, a view which I accept is an unpromising basis for a specific law. Had the law regarding obscenity remained as stringent as in Stephen's day (which, fortunately, it has not), I would have no qualms about consigning all 'blasphemy' to that jurisdiction; but obscene blasphemy requires to be restrained in a stricter manner than commonplace obscenity.

The reason for the most guarded use of the law in protecting religious sensitivities is not that those issues treated by religion are 'subjective' or trivial, but rather that they are of profound and universal concern. In religion, particular beliefs are an invitation (whether deliberately offered, or taken up, or not) to everyone to consider the deepest questions of our existence and destiny. Atheists may not have religious images to protect, but they share this concern; Marx and Nietzsche are theologians of a sort. Because this concern is universal, and because religious ideas can affirm or deny one another, offence is endemic to religion. But although 'offence' cannot be absolutely distinguished from other injuries, it is also an integral part of the vitality of intellect and spirit. St Paul, who once 'was consenting unto' the death of the blasphemer Stephen, was well aware that the paradox he preached was offensive (a foolishness, a stumbling-block) and blasphemously offensive to the world's ideas of wisdom and holiness. In arguing that the crucial consideration for the criminal law is not merely the degree of offence, but the character of the offensive matter as an argument, I give regard not only to the pugnacious connotation of 'offence' (and the implication that a fair 'defence' should be possible), but also to the conditions of spiritual vigour.

Notes

I am most obliged to Professor D. D. Raphael for pointing out many errors in the first draft of this essay.

1 See W. K. Jordan, *The Development of Religious Toleration in England*, vol. III, London, 1965.
2 Useful works for the history of the crime of balsphemy are: C. M. Aspland, *The Law of Blasphemy*, London, 1884; C. Bradlaugh, *The Laws relating to Blasphemy and Heresy*, London, 1878; H. Bradlaugh-Bonner, *Penalties upon Opinion*, 3rd edn, London, 1934; G. D. Nokes, *A History of the Crime of Blasphemy*, London, 1928.
3 Quoted in H. Bradlaugh-Bonner, op. cit., 30–1.
4 Quoted in *Gay News*, no. 162, 8–21 March 1979, 10–11.
5 Sir Norman Anderson (a lawyer, and former chairman of the Laity of the General Synod who advised Dr Runcie) stated in a letter to the *Church Times*, 12 February 1982: 'What has in fact been suggested is a law which would penalise the publication of "matter which vilifies, ridicules or insults" the fundamental beliefs of Christianity – or, indeed of any other "religious group", "knowing that this is likely to insult or outrage their feelings, to provoke a breach of the peace or disturb public order and tranquillity". It would *not* in any way restrict freedom of speech about any matter of faith or practice, provided the publication kept within the bounds of decent debate or controversy.'
6 For analysis of the relation between the 'offence principle' and the law, see Joel Feinberg, *Social Philosophy*, Englewood Cliffs, New Jersey, 1973, and Feinberg's discussion, 'Harmless immoralities and offensive nuisances', in N. S. Care and T. K. Trelogan (eds), *Issues in Law and Morality*, Cleveland, Ohio, 1973; D. Van de Veer, 'Coercive restraint of offensive action', *Philosophy and Public Affairs*, 8, 1979. The matter is discussed with specific reference to the blasphemy law in Peter Jones's excellent article, 'Blasphemy, offensiveness and law', *British Journal of Political Science*, 10, 1980.
7 The ambiguities associated with the concept of harm are explored in the essay by John Horton in this volume.
8 Notions concerning respect (especially 'respect to persons') occur frequently in arguments about toleration, and they figure in the essays by Thomas Baldwin and Albert Weale in this volume.

9   *The Guardian*, 12 January 1982.

10   e.g. Milton in *Areopagitica* says, 'Where a man hath . . . drawn forth his reasons as it were a battle ranged: scattered and defeated all objections in his way; calls out his adversary into the plain, offers him the advantage of wind and sun, if he please, only that he may try the matter by dint of argument: for his opponents then to skulk, to lay ambushments . . . is but weakness and cowardice in the wars of Truth.'

11   A. Schweitzer, *The Quest for the Historical Jesus*, London 1910, 4.

12   Quoted in *Gay News*, op. cit.

13   J. F. Stephen, 'Blasphemy and blasphemous libel', *Fortnightly Review*, CCVII, new series, March 1884.

14   Rudolph Otto, *The Idea of the Holy*, London, 2nd edn 1950.

15   In the sermon 'The Divine Name' in Paul Tillich, *The Boundaries of Our Being*, London, 1973.

16   *Salisbury and Winchester Journal*, quoted in Gerald S. Hawkins, *Stonehenge Decoded*, London, 1975.

5

Harm, offence and censorship

SUSAN MENDUS

And she increased her whoredom when she saw men portrayed
upon the wall, the images of the Chaldeans portrayed with
vermilion. Gilded with girdles upon their loins, exceeding in
dyed attire upon their heads, all of them princes to look to after
the manner of the Babylonians of Chaldea ... And as soon as
she saw them with her eyes, she doted upon them and sent
messengers unto them into Chaldea. And the Babylonians came
to her into the bed of love, and they defiled her with their
whoredom.[1]

This is, I believe, the first recorded case of corruption by pictorial
material; the corruption of Aholibah as related in Ezekiel. It is not,
however, the last and the belief that certain material may corrupt,
may be a spiritual and moral poison, is still current and, indeed,
is embodied in the 1959 Obscene Publications Act, which states
that an article is obscene

if its effect or, where the article comprises two or more distinct
items, the effect of any one of its items is, if taken as a whole,
such as to tend to deprave and corrupt persons who are likely,
having regard to all relevant circumstances, to read, see or hear
the matter contained or embodied in it.

To this extent, the present law is one which construes obscene
material as potentially corrupting and which concerns itself with
the protection of the individual from such a corrupting influence.
In recent years, however, and particularly in the 'permissive' days
of the 1960s and 1970s, such a view has been thought to be outdated

and this, combined with the notorious difficulties inherent in interpreting and applying the 1959 Act, led the then Home Secretary, in 1977, to set up a Committee under the chairmanship of Professor Bernard Williams to 'review the laws concerning obscenity, indecency and violence in publications, displays and entertainments in England and Wales, except in the field of broadcasting, and to review the arrangements for film censorship in England and Wales and to make recommendations'.[2] Reporting in 1979, the Committee announced:

> One of the first decisions we took was to escape from the words which have been a part of the law for so long. The 'tendency to deprave and corrupt' and the words 'obscene' and 'indecent' were, we concluded, now useless. (9.21)

Instead, the Committee offered a criterion in terms of offence, proposing that material should be suppressed only if it caused harm, and restricted where,

> not consisting of the written word, [it] is such that its unrestricted availability is offensive to reasonable people by reason of the manner in which it portrays, deals with or relates to violence, cruelty or horror, or sexual, faecal or urinary functions, or genital organs. (9.36)

Indeed the Committee urged that the 'main aim' of the law should be 'to restrict pornography so that it will not be offensive to the public' (9.7). Its recommendations thus urge a move from the protection of the moral welfare of the individual to protection of the individual's sensibilities: the view that certain kinds of material are a spiritual and moral poison is abandoned in favour of the view that certain sorts of material cause offence to reasonable people and that reasonable people have a right that their sensibilities be protected by the law.

The 1959 Act and the Report of the Williams Committee both individually and jointly give rise to important questions about the grounds on which we may properly restrict or suppress certain sorts of material: should we ask, 'Is this material evil? Will it deprave or corrupt?', or should we rather ask, 'What harm will it do? Will reasonable people reasonably be offended by it?' While the 1959 Act urges the former questions upon us, the Report of the Williams Committee urges the latter. In what follows I aim to present a comparative analysis of the 1959 Act and the Report of the Williams Committee. My argument will be that the present Act, despite its inadequacies, incorporates an important insight into the status of objections to pornographic or obscene material and that this insight is one which the Williams Committee lacks. Moreover, I shall try to show that any attempt to 'liberalize' the law by couching it in terms of offence will ultimately fail to do justice to the views of those who object to pornography: the liberal who advocates toleration in this area standardly provides arguments which can convince only those who are already persuaded. To say this, however, is not to deny the problems inherent in the present law. Indeed, to reach these conclusions at all it will be necessary to see precisely why the 1959 Obscene Publications Act has been thought to be 'confused, impractical and intellectually hypocritical'.[3] I begin, therefore, with a discussion of the 1959 Act and of the problems inherent in it. My hope is that this discussion will show both why it was thought to be important to recommend changes and why the changes recommended by Williams are ultimately unsatisfactory.

The 1959 Obscene Publications Act is an amendment of the 1868 Hicklin test of obscenity. Both the Act and the test define 'obscene' as 'tending to deprave and corrupt' and it is this definition which has proved a veritable minefield for judges, lawyers and publishers alike. Lord Wilberforce, in *DPP* v. *Whyte* (1972), despairingly concluded that

> Such words [deprave and corrupt] provide a formula which cannot in practice be applied ... I have serious doubts whether the Act will continue to be workable in this way and whether it will produce tolerable results. The present is, or in any rational system ought to be, a simple case, yet the illogical and unscientific character of the Act has forced the judges into untenable positions.

The basic problem lies in the fact that the 1959 Act contains no interpretation section and, in the absence of this, judges have varied dramatically in the advice they have given to juries: the publisher of an illustrated booklet entitled *Scanties* appealed against his conviction on the ground that the judge had not told the jury that

101

they should be satisfied that the article was something more than merely shocking or vulgar. On appeal, however, Lord Goddard declared that it did not matter what the judge had or had not told the jury, 'one had only to pick up the book in order to feel quite certain that no jury could conceivably fail to convict'.[4] By contrast, in the *Oz* case it was held on appeal that the judge's direction that 'obscene' might include what is filthy, loathsome, indecent and lewd was 'a very serious and substantial mis-direction'.[5] Moreover, even where it has been agreed that 'deprave and corrupt' must mean more than simply 'shock and disgust', it has still been unclear whether such depravity and corruption must manifest itself in behaviour. In the case of *DPP* v. *Whyte* (1972) the Lords held that material might corrupt even if its only influence were to arouse thoughts of 'a most impure and libidinous character', whereas in *Knuller* v. *DPP* (1973) the Law Lords emphasized that the effect of publication must be to produce real social evil, 'constituting a serious menace to the community and going beyond immoral suggestion and persuasion'. Difficulties of the above sort are, moreover, compounded by the fact that the Act insists only that material shall *tend* to deprave and corrupt, not that it actually *shall* deprave and corrupt. In this connection juries, having no appeal to expert opinion, may well flounder, and indeed it is the difficulty of interpretation and application of the tendency test which has brought the present Act into disrepute. I turn now, therefore, to various suggested interpretations of the 'deprave and corrupt' test and to the question of whether there is any inter-pretation of that test which will render the present law workable.

In a recent article on this topic, A. D. Woozley has noted that there are two main senses in which it may be said that A tends to ϕ.[6] The first of these senses is the frequency sense; the second the likelihood sense. In the frequency sense 'A tends to ϕ' means that more often than not A ϕs; in the likelihood sense 'A tends to ϕ' means that probably A will ϕ. The difference between these two is that the former is an empirical frequency statement; the second a statement (non-empirical) of probability. In the second, like-lihood, sense, the truth of 'A tends to ϕ' is compatible with A's hardly ever ϕing, because of the counter-balancing effects of other influences. In this sense 'cyanide tends to poison' is true, even though it hardly ever does poison anybody because we are careful about how we handle it. Comparably, we might claim that certain obscene or pornographic material tends to deprave and corrupt, even though it hardly ever does deprave or corrupt anybody, because of the influence of family life, long runs, cold showers and so on. The difficulty here, however, is that of providing evidence that material tends to deprave and corrupt in this sense. The reason we can say of certain drugs that they tend or are likely to poison even though they have never actually done so, is because of their resemblance to other drugs which have poisoned. In the obscenity case, however, we have nothing to compare the material with except other material whose corrupting influence is equally in doubt. If we knew that a particular film had corrupted, it might be plausible to say that a book consisting of 'stills' from the film would be likely to corrupt, but the book's resemblance to the film cannot count as evidence for its corrupting influence unless the film has already been shown to have the corrupting effect, and in trying to show the latter we return, full circle, to the original problem. The Model Penal Code's criticism of the English law was simply that there was no evidence that people who indulged in reading the material complained of engaged, as a consequence, in conduct different from that which they would have engaged in anyway.

Thus, where 'tend' is taken in either of these two senses it is difficult to see how jury members can ever pronounce on the question of whether an article tends to deprave and corrupt. This fact alone has meant that juries in obscenity trials have refrained from asking themselves the unanswerable question, 'Does this tend to deprave and corrupt?' in favour of the easier question, 'Am I shocked by it?' In doing this they run the risk of convicting unfairly, since it is far from obvious that everything which shocks and disgusts also depraves and corrupts. Indeed, one successful defence rested its case upon the claim that the book in question was so disgusting as to have no tendency to deprave or corrupt at all. 'One vindicates a book by its capacity to induce vomiting.' This claim was central to the defence in the *Oz* trial and was accepted by the Court of Appeal when the Lord Chief Justice held that

the learned trial judge never really put over to the jury that the proposition central to the defence case was that certain illustrations could be so disgusting and filthy that they would not deprave and corrupt, but rather would tend to cause people to revolt from anything of that kind.[7]

On the other hand, when juries have assiduously concentrated on the words of the statute they have, not surprisingly, found themselves incapable of deciding whether the material has a tendency to deprave and corrupt and have, therefore, been reluctant to convict at all. Indeed, it is hard to see how anything could be convicted, since the tendency to deprave and corrupt must be proven by the normal criterion in criminal law, i.e. beyond reasonable doubt.

Thus, where 'tend' is taken in either of the two senses mentioned above (the frequency sense and the likelihood sense) the jury will invariably find themselves being asked a question which they simply cannot answer. They should, therefore, acquit. If they do not acquit, it will most probably be because they have not asked themselves the right question. Woozley suggests that there is a third sense of 'tend' according to which it can be shown that certain sorts of material tend to deprave and corrupt and which does not encounter the problems raised by the first two interpretations. This sense of 'tend' is that used by Mill in his *System of Logic* and (more oddly) in his evidence of 1871 for the Commission on the Administration of Contagious Diseases Act. (It is also, Woozley suggests, the sense of 'tend' in his claim that 'actions are right in proportion as they tend to promote happiness'.) On this interpretation 'tend' is divorced both from statements of frequency and from statements of likelihood. To say here that A tends to ϕ is to ascribe to A some causal property such that its having that causal property is consistent with its seldom, if ever, producing the effect and with its not being likely to produce the effect. Anscombe and Geach tell us that

> Mill's use of 'tendency' has nothing to do with what usually happens; for he says that all heavy bodies tend to fall, although balloons do not usually fall. Similarly, he is not speaking of what is likely to happen, for there is not the least likelihood (he said) that a one ton pull will raise a body weighing three tons.[8]

We should not, therefore, think of tendencies as mere potentialities – 'a tendency is somehow actual, not a mere "would happen if" '.

Perhaps we need here a sense of tendency similar to Locke's 'power'.[9] In this sense of 'tend' it may be true both that A tends to ϕ and that it never has ϕed nor is it likely to ϕ. Thus it may be true both that a particular item tends to deprave and corrupt and that it never has corrupted anyone nor is it likely ever to corrupt anyone. More particularly, its having this tendency is consistent with there being no evidence either in support of or against the proposition that it usually had or was likely to have such an effect.

The difficulty with Woozley's interpretation however is that it seems to depend upon an analogy between the corrupting influence of obscene material and the poisonous effect of certain drugs. It may well be true that

> The poison which I pour into the town's water reservoir does have a tendency to make the water from the reservoir unfit or unsafe to drink, even though there is no danger that it will, because of counteractive factors.[10]

Here it may be said that I have poisoned the water supply, even if I have not made it poisonous. But we can, I think, say that only because we have already identified the substance as poison. We say that certain substances are poisonous partly because of their similarity to other substances which we know to be poisonous and those other substances we know to be poisonous because they have poisoned in the past. In other words, this third sense of 'tend' is parasitic on senses (1) and (2). In the case of pornographic or obscene material, however, we cannot show that anything tends to deprave and corrupt in either the first or the second sense and therefore we cannot show that it does so in this third sense of 'tend'. The distinction between A's tending to ϕ and A's being likely to or frequently ϕing can be drawn only in cases where there is already evidence that A or something very similar to A does tend to ϕ in one of the first two senses. Again, Geach and Anscombe:

> Even though the other tendencies involved in a given situation prevent the actual fulfilment of a given tendency, its presence will always make a difference to what actually happens; and the procedure of scientific explanation is to infer natural tendencies from what actually happens, and then predict what will happen

from the natural tendencies of the agencies believed to be operative. This procedure demands either the physical isolation of agents or the mental analysis of their joint results. What characterises a given kind of natural agent is not so much actual operatives as tendencies; but some tendencies come into effect to a recognisable extent in spite of interference – otherwise we could never discern any tendencies at all; since a tendency is specifiable only by the operation to which it is a tendency.[11]

Thus, although we may say that cyanide tends to poison, this is only because we know that in some cases it has poisoned; we infer from what actually happens and then predict what will happen. But where, as in the case of pornographic material, there is no evidence that anything of that kind (assuming that we can sensibly talk of a class of pornographic material) has ever corrupted, it is difficult to see how we could substantiate a claim that this pornographic material now corrupts or tends to corrupt. In the case of pornographic material this sense of 'tend' appears not to be applicable, and in any case, even if it could be shown that certain sorts of material did tend to deprave and corrupt in this sense, the fact that they never actually do so, and are unlikely to do so, might well render laws prohibiting the publication of such material unnecessary and pointless. Why, after all, should the law concern itself with material which is not likely to corrupt anyone, and does not corrupt anyone? Of course, it is not true that the law's only concern is with actual effects on people: the law on attempt is not concerned with actual effects, but that law does import a *mens rea* condition which is not present in the case of obscenity laws. The latter are not concerned with harmful intent and if, as Woozley suggests, they are not concerned with harmful effect, then what are they concerned with?

These and related difficulties in interpreting the Obscene Publications Act have led lawyers and laymen alike to suggest abandoning the 'deprave and corrupt' test in favour of some other. The report of the Williams Committee notes that in its investigations it found that 'the "indecent" or "obscene" test had some defenders; the "deprave and corrupt" test, the most basic idea of the most important law, had none' (2.14); and it goes on to recommend that such terms as 'obscene', 'indecent' , 'deprave and corrupt' should be abandoned as having outlived their usefulness and that the

> law rest partly on the basis of harm caused by or involved in the existence of the material (this alone justifies prohibition) and partly on the basis of the public's legitimate interest in not being offended by the display and availability of material (this can justify no more than the imposition of restrictions designed to protect the ordinary citizen from unreasonable offence). (9.7 and 10.2)

The effect of these proposals, if implemented, would be to shift the emphasis of the obscenity laws from the protection of morals to the protection of feelings. The law would no longer concern itself with the moral character of individuals exposed to pornographic material, but rather with protecting people from feelings of offence caused by the material. In many ways this shift of emphasis is practical and laudable; numerous efforts have been made, both here and abroad, to improve obscenity laws by tinkering with the definition of 'obscene' and all have failed dismally. In the American Supreme Court, Justice Brennan concluded despairingly

> Although we have assumed that obscenity does exist and that we know it when we see it, we are manifestly unable to describe it in advance except by reference to concepts so elusive that they fail to distinguish clearly between protected and unprotected speech.[12]

Nevertheless, even if attempts to define obscenity are abandoned it is not clear that laws phrased in terms of what will offend will fare any better. For Brennan also declared in the same speech that 'the line between communications which offend and those which do not is too blurred to identify criminal conduct'.[13] So it is not obvious that an offence test will prove to be more reliable than the 'deprave and corrupt' test. My main concern here, however, is with the way in which the recommendations of the Report shift the concern of the law from the protection of the consumer's moral welfare to the protection of individual sensibilities. Such a shift would undeniably result in a discrepancy between the concern of the law and the concern of many of those seeking protection under the law: for most people who favour stringent laws governing pornography do so not because they wish not to be shocked, offended or outraged, but because they believe such material to be morally damaging to those who are exposed to it. Now it is already true that such discrepancy exists elsewhere in our legal system, most notably in the case of the blasphemy laws. Peter Jones has pointed out that in the *Gay News* trial the law's concern was with prevention and protection from offence, whereas Mrs Mary Whitehouse's concern was with 'the protection of the Lord'.[14] So it might be argued that, since we already have at least one comparable case in which the concern of the law differs from the concern of those appealing to the law, the recommendations of the Williams Report are not automatically rendered worthless by this observation. I shall argue, however, that there are independent internal reasons for thinking that the recommendations are inadequate and point-missing. Primary amongst these reasons is the Report's failure adequately to justify its preference for 'offence' as a criterion: at 9.3 the Committee urges construing pornographic material as a nuisance and as something requiring control for that reason. However, in the very same section they change their ground, insisting that pornography should be the subject of law because it may otherwise constitute an invasion of privacy, and they go on to talk as though the nuisance argument and the privacy argument were one and the same. There are, however, important differences between these two and I believe that the oddities inherent in the Report spring from a failure to make these distinctions. If I am right and the Report does sometimes concern itself with privacy rather than nuisance, then the consequences will be not only that in some cases the law's concern will be different from the concerns of the individuals who seek protection from the law, it will also be (to make a point Williams himself makes in a different context) that when the law comes up with the right answer it may do so for the wrong reasons.

The point here is, I think, this: objections to obscene or pornographic material are of a sort similar to objections to nuisances, for example to pollution or destruction of beautiful stretches of countryside, and these objections are quite distinct from objections to invasion of privacy in at least two senses: firstly, in the case of nuisance the recommendation to avert one's gaze is inappropriate and, secondly, the harm caused is a harm to no one in particular, but to society in general. By contrast, in the privacy case, every invasion of privacy is an invasion of *someone's* privacy and where privacy is at issue then that may be obtained by averting one's gaze or locking oneself in one's room. I do not object to obscene or pornographic material because it constitutes a breach of privacy any more than I object to raw sewage being pumped into a nearby river because *that* constitutes a breach of privacy. Thus, in neither case is the foisting or unwillingness charge the appropriate one, nor is the instruction to avert my gaze consoling.[15]

The recognition of this, however, may lead us to construe those who object to pornography as akin to conservationists, and the analogy drawn above between the anti-pornographer and the conservationist brings us back full circle to Woozley's suggestion that obscene or pornographic material may be said to tend to deprave and corrupt, even if it never has corrupted anyone and is unlikely ever to corrupt anyone. More importantly, it resurrects the original analogy drawn by Woozley between pornographic material and poison in the water supply. But now we are, perhaps, in a position to make better sense of Woozley's claim. The present law and the Report of the Williams Committee both insist upon construing the 'deprave and corrupt' test causally. Once this is conceded it becomes well-nigh impossible to provide the hard empirical evidence required to show that any particular material does have the corrupting tendency in question. However, as we have seen, abandoning that test in favour of a test in terms of what actually offends people is no solution, for this latter test ignores the essential character of the objection to pornography, construing the situation as one in which privacy and protection from offended sensibilities are at issue, when in fact the issue is more akin to those in which environmental questions are at stake. To quote one commentator; 'the case against pornography is confused by the cause-and-effect talk. Pornography does not *cause* depravity and corruption, it *is* depravity and corruption.'[16] In this sense, then, the opponent of pornography will not see the point of trying to prove causally that pornography depraves and corrupts, nor need he argue that anyone who reads pornographic material will, as a consequence, engage in deviant and unacceptable behaviour: the depravity lies in the very involvement with pornographic material, and is independent of any subsequent behaviour engaged in.

It may seem that if that is what is involved, then the opponents of pornography must either provide a workable legal definition of the class of pornographic material, or else admit that the law has no place here. I will not enter into the thorny question of the definition of pornography,[17] but will rather quote, as an example, a case in which it is precisely argued that certain kinds of material are themselves depraved and corrupted.

Since the liberal and permissive days of the 1960s and 1970s, public opinion on the question of pornography has altered dramatically: the pendulum has swung against toleration and in favour of censorship, and in the vanguard have been members of the feminist movement. Andrea Dworkin's now notorious claim that 'pornography *is* violence against women'[18] has been criticized as extravagant and exaggerated. Be that as it may, it provides an example of the non-causal nature of the anti-pornographer's case. It may or may not be the case that pornography causes or results in or encourages violence against women, but to say that it does is to be honour-bound to produce the empirical evidence or remain silent. Dworkin's belief, and her complaint, is that even where such empirical evidence is lacking, pornography nevertheless is *itself* a form of violence against women, since it exploits and subjugates them. This kind of complaint highlights the inadequacy for anyone like Dworkin of pornography laws which seek merely to protect the unwitting and frail from feelings of offence, for her complaint is not that *she* wishes not to have to encounter such material, but that such material is corrupt whether she encounters it or not. She wants it not to exist.

This is, I believe, the truth in the present law: pornography does not *tend* to deprave and corrupt, it is depraved and corrupt and for that very reason the attempt to justify pornography laws by appeal to a right to privacy is doomed from the start. Where the issue is one of privacy I may guarantee that by averting my gaze. Privacy may be obtained by restricting pornographic material to special shops. But since the objection is not an objection to invasion of privacy, these recommendations are point-missing and irrelevant. Moreover, the analogy between the pornography question and environmental questions is strengthened by the insistence that pornography actually destroys something of value. In this case, the position of women as human beings on an equal footing with men is undermined and threatened by the proliferation of pornographic material which portrays women as objects or as inferiors. The claim that environmental threats destroy something of value, whereas pornographic literature does not destroy works of literary merit is thus contentious, for it is a large part of the feminist argument against pornography that it *does* destroy something of value, namely the position of women within the society as a whole. And again, it is important to recognize that this charge is not based upon, nor does it need, the proof that any *one* individual has been corrupted or harmed: as in the environmental case, the harm done is a harm to society in general and not to any one individual in particular.

In advancing this argument I do not thereby indicate my agreement with it. Whether I agree with the feminist complaint is largely irrelevant here; what *is* relevant, however, is the fact that this is the complaint and it is a complaint which has nothing to do with feelings of offence. Of course feminists *are* offended by pornography, but their offence springs from the belief that such material is corrupt. It follows, therefore, that what they want is not that they should not have to encounter pornography, but that there should be no pornography. It follows too that their feelings of offence will cease only when pornography ceases, not when access to pornography is restricted to those who want it.

If the central thought informing those who wish to ban pornography is that pornography is akin to pollution, is indeed morally polluting, there remains the question whether it is the proper business of the law to act as guardian of the moral standards of society. Many have thought not and, if they are right, then the above argument will do nothing to advance the cause either of feminism or of the Festival of Light. Nevertheless, it will serve to highlight how deep are the differences between those who favour censorship and those who do not. To attempt, in the name of toleration, to minimize those differences is at best naive and at worst hypocritical, for ultimately the man who professes to be tolerant in this area may end up tolerating all those and only those who share his views.[19]

111

Notes

1   Ezekiel 23; 14–17.
2   *Report of the Committee on Obscenity and Film Censorship*, Cmnd. 7772, Para. 1.1, London, 1979; hereafter references to the report are by paragraph number and in parentheses.
3   Polly Toynbee as quoted in J. Sutherland, *Offensive Literature: Censorship in Britain 1960–1982*, London, 1982, 179.
4   C. H. R. Rolph, *Books in the Dock*, London, 1969, 63.
5   *R. v. Anderson* (1972), as quoted in G. Robertson, *Obscenity*, London, 1979, 48–9.
6   A. D. Woozley, 'The tendency to deprave and corrupt', *Law and Philosophy*, 1, 1982.
7   *R. v. Anderson* (1972), as quoted in G. Robertson, op. cit., 52.
8   G. E. M. Anscombe and P. T. Geach, *Three Philosophers*, Oxford, 1963, 103.
9   John Locke, *Essay on Human Understanding*, II, viii, 8, 10, 23.
10 Woozley, op. cit., 231.
11 Anscombe and Geach, op. cit., 104.
12 *Pairs Adult Theatre* v. *Slaton*, 1973, as quoted in G. Robertson, op. cit., 310.
13 ibid.
14 P. Jones, 'Blasphemy, offensiveness and law', *British Journal of Political Science*, 10, 1980, 139, n. 45.
15 See N. MacCormick, 'Privacy and obscenity', in R. Dhavan and C. Davies (eds), *Censorship and Obscenity*, London, 1978.
16 I. Robinson, *The Survival of English*, Cambridge, 1973, 165. I am grateful to John Horton for bringing my attention to Robinson's argument.
17 For a proposed definition see *Report of the Committee on Obscenity and Film Censorship*, Para. 8.2.
18 A. Dworkin, *Pornography: Men Possessing Women*, London, 1981.
19 I am especially grateful to John Horton and Peter Nicholson for their extensive and very helpful comments on an earlier draft of this paper.

6

Toleration, morality and harm

JOHN HORTON

A belief common to much of both recent political and legal theory and popular moral and political thought is that a necessary, though not sufficient, condition for the legal restriction of any activity is its being harmful. Furthermore, in what might loosely be called the liberal tradition, it is primarily the prevention of harm to others which has been thought to be the proper concern of the law. Actions and practices which are not harmful, and for the liberal those where such harm as there is largely affects only the agent, should be tolerated. The classic statement of this view, of course, is that of J. S. Mill:

> The object of this essay is to assert one very simple principle as entitled to govern absolutely the dealings of society with the individual in the way of compulsion and control, whether the means used be physical force in the form of legal penalties or the moral coercion of public opinion. That principle is that the sole end for which mankind are warranted, individually or collectively, in interfering with the liberty of action of any one of their number is self-protection. That the only purpose for which power can be rightfully exercised over a member of a civilised community, against his will, is to prevent harm to others.[1]

As Mill makes clear, in this passage and elsewhere in *On Liberty*, his concern is not merely with legal prohibition but also with what he calls 'the moral coercion of public opinion' which makes his principle of broader relevance than the proper scope of law. However, despite its claimed simplicity, Mill's principle has been subject to a variety of interpretations as to its meaning. One problem which has occasioned this variety of interpretations is Mill's conception of harm and its role in the application of his principle. The importance of this issue should be apparent, for if Mill's principle is to be of much practical use in identifying a range of conduct which should be tolerated, then there needs to be some uncontroversial way of distinguishing those actions and practices which are harmful from those which are not. In what follows I will suggest that there is no uncontroversial way in which such a distinction can be drawn and, therefore, any attempt to justify toleration which relies on such a supposedly agreed distinction is likely to be seriously defective. I begin with a brief consideration of this problem as it arises in Mill.

A common objection to Mill's principle is that it depends upon an untenable distinction between self- and other-regarding actions, for there are, so it is claimed, no significant actions which do not affect others. However, much modern scholarship has been concerned to show that this objection is misconceived and C. L. Ten has recently argued that the distinction between self- and other-regarding relates not to classes of actions but rather to types of reason for restricting actions.[2] In Ten's view Mill is arguing that:

> Some reasons for intervention are relevant while others are not. Intervention in order to prevent harm to others is always relevant but one is never justified in interfering simply because one dislikes the conduct, or strongly disapproves of it. The absoluteness of Mill's barrier against intervention is raised only against certain reasons for intervention which are often invoked.[3]

Thus, on this view, Mill is not concerned to distinguish two mutually exclusive types of actions but rather two types of reason for interfering with an individual's actions. The crucial distinction is between arguments that invoke 'harm to others' as a reason for interference with some action, and arguments which cite only the dislike or disapproval of those seeking to interfere. Whatever its precise merits as an interpretation of the argument of *On Liberty*, and this is not an issue that can be entered into here, Ten's account brings out even more clearly than traditional interpretations the crucial role of the concept of harm in the formulation of Mill's principle.[4] On this view of it, Mill's argument requires that the harmful character of some action be specifiable independently of attitudes of dislike or disapproval. Of course in some instances this will be entirely unproblematic for there are many activities that we may dislike or disapprove of yet not think harmful. However, there are other cases which are much less straightforward and present serious problems for Mill's principle.

The first difficulty is that if Mill is to have any hope of succeeding in his aim of protecting a substantial range of conduct from the interference of others, then it is especially important that he not regard as harm the distress caused to a person merely through that person's belief in the wrongness of some line of conduct. Some persons, for example, believe the public display of sexually explicit materials is wrong and such public displays cause them to be shocked and offended. Unless the psychological distress involved in such shock and offence can be shown not to be harmful, it will provide a legitimate reason for legally restricting the public display of such sexually explicit materials. The problem here is that a person's beliefs about what is right and wrong, proper and improper, offensive and inoffensive, may be causally connected to what distresses him. Unless there is a compelling reason for rejecting the commonsense view that such distress is harmful, it will often not be possible to make a clear distinction between arguments that invoke harm to others and those which adduce only disapproval or dislike as a reason for not tolerating a particular action or practice. This is a serious difficulty. A second and more profound objection is that the problem for Mill is not merely that the harm may be *caused* through others' beliefs about the wrongness of some action, but that judgements about what is harmful are also, at least in part, *constituted* by such beliefs. What is conceived as harmful is not, as I shall be concerned to argue, independent of particular moral perspectives and, for this reason, the concept of harm is peculiarly ill-fitted to fulfil the function Mill requires of it. In short, what is thought to be harmful depends upon what is held to be valuable, and in so far as what is thought to be valuable is a matter of disagreement and controversy, so is what is conceived as harmful.

The extent to which Mill was aware of these problems is questionable, but there have been some ingenious attempts to reconstruct from this work possible replies to them.[5] By far the most plausible of these rest on some form of utilitarian interpretation of the meaning of 'harm to others'.[6] However, though such an interpretation would provide answers of a sort to these difficulties, it would do so only at the cost of making those answers much more controversial than Mill's tone in *On Liberty* suggests. For utilitarianism, despite the exaggerated claims of some of its proponents, is not synonymous with morality, but at best only one moral perspective among others. I say 'at best' because there are many different forms of utilitarianism and deep problems concerning the internal coherence and adequacy of all of them.[7] Furthermore, since my interest is in the problem of the role of harm in delimiting an area of conduct which should be tolerated rather than in the exegesis of *On Liberty*, I shall not pursue the discussion of Mill any further. The crucial issue of general significance is whether or not there is a plausible conception of harm which is neutral between different moral points of view. The importance of this issue is not limited to the interpretation of Mill but raises difficult problems about the basis of legislation generally and the nature of liberalism in particular. For liberals, especially, have espoused the view mentioned earlier that the principal reason for legally prohibiting individuals from engaging in a particular course of action is that it would cause or constitute a harm to another person either directly, or indirectly through some public harm. However, the liberal is also characteristically committed to the view that the law should aim to be neutral between competing conceptions of the good and differing moral perspectives.[8] Of course it is rarely thought, and then only by the most naive, that this neutrality can in any sense be complete, for it is, to put it mildly, hard to envisage how any legal system could be neutral between all the moral beliefs and practices which history and social anthropology have made known. Rather, the liberal's argument is that the basis of legislation should be the prevention of harm to others, and that within this limitation the law should not seek to enforce or protect any particular moral point of view. However, the cogency of the liberal's position will depend upon the plausibility of an uncontroversial conception of harm, for, if what is thought to be harmful is internally connected to particular moral perspectives, then the liberal's position can be seen to be deeply flawed. It is the contention of this essay that this is indeed the case and that the supposed moral neutrality of liberalism is almost always compromised when it resorts to the concept of harm. Thus the problem which infects Mill's account of 'harm to others' is one which faces liberalism more generally.

In many respects the argument developed here is familiar,[9] but its force is usually insufficiently appreciated. For it seriously undermines the practical utility of the frequently heard appeal that a given activity should be tolerated because it is harmless. Certainly if an activity is harmless that may be a strong reason for tolerating it, but the judgement whether or not it is harmless is a much more complicated issue than is frequently allowed. In particular, the harmlessness of an activity often cannot be established independently of the moral point of view from which such a judgement is made, and therefore it is most likely that where there is serious disagreement about the moral quality of any activity there will also be disagreement about whether it is harmful. If this claim is correct then appeals to what is or is not harmful in an attempt to reconcile (or at least produce mutual toleration between) those with conflicting moral viewpoints are likely to be either ineffective or bogus.

The immense flexibility in the application of the concept of harm can easily be established. Even the most cursory survey of moral and political debate would reveal the variety of what is or is not considered harmful. At times it would seem almost anything can be conceived of as harmful. Thus Mr Norman Tebbit could say of some anti-war plays presented to school children in Chingford that they were 'at best irrelevant and at the worst decidedly harmful'.[10] On the other hand, Mr Derek Malcolm could write of the controversial whipping scene in Michael Winner's film remake of *The Wicked Lady* that it seemed 'harmless enough nowadays'.[11] One does not have to look very far to see all manner of activities charged with being harmful by their critics while their adherents defend them as at least harmless or even positively beneficial. The debate about pornography provides a particularly clear example of this phenomenon and, as the Williams Committee on Obscenity and Film Censorship noted in their Report, virtually everyone who gave evidence and made suggestions to them couched their arguments in 'the language of "harm"'', even though there was widespread disagreement 'about what might count as harm'.[12] Thus, while there is much agreement that the question whether or not some activity is harmful is of crucial relevance in deciding whether or not it should be legally restricted, there is less agreement about what activities are harmful. Of course some claims about the allegedly harmful or harmless character of an activity may be disingenuous and may be shown to be so, but this is clearly untrue of many such disputes. Is there any way in which such authentic disputes may be resolved?

One likely response to what has been claimed is that it has greatly exaggerated the extent of disagreement about what is harmful, and it might be maintained that though there is some disagreement at the margins, the central cases are clear. One version of this view is expressed by J. R. Lucas:

> To be harmful, a thing must be something that most people do not want, and which we think that they are right not to want. It is part of our common set of values, which we are prepared to affirm, irrespective of what any particular person wants or claims to want. The paradigm cases are death, bodily injury, and imprisonment. Most people not merely want to avoid these evils, but are convinced that they are evil, and will not be persuaded otherwise. No matter how much a man protests that so far as he is concerned he does not mind whether he is killed, mutilated, or incarcerated, we do not take him seriously, and we continue to regard it as harming him if he is killed, mutilated or put in prison.[13]

Lucas's discussion of harm is in many respects both subtle and sensitive to some of the complexities of the concept. In particular he is aware that:

> What is regarded as harmful depends upon the common values of the community and the ideal patterns of life, cherished by it ... The concept of harm is thus an elusive one, although the paradigm cases are clear. It is therefore a dangerous one for the political philosopher to use. The paradigm cases give it a spurious air of certainty and definiteness, while the extended ones are in fact uncertain and indefinite.[14]

Furthermore, for reasons similar to those given earlier, Lucas is also highly sceptical of the use of the concept of harm in Mill's formulation of his principle. However, even Lucas's cautious formulation in terms of paradigm cases is unduly optimistic about the degree of agreement there is or need be about what is harmful. There are three points to be made about these paradigm cases of harm. First, even if Lucas were right about there being agreed harms, it should be noted just how few they are and the extent to which they are primarily material harms. Secondly, again conceding the substance of Lucas's claim that his paradigm cases are indeed harmful, it does not follow that they need be regarded as of greater weight than other harms which are not paradigmatic. In short, their status as paradigms does not ensure that such harms will always be viewed as the most serious of harms. Thirdly, the very status of these harms as paradigmatic might be doubted. I shall elaborate each of these points more fully though they will be taken in reverse order.

It might seem peculiarly perverse to doubt that death, bodily injury and imprisonment are harmful. Surely, it will be claimed, if we can agree that anything is harmful then we can agree that these are harmful. However, there is at least some scope for reasoned and intelligible disagreement, though there are no doubt limits to such disagreement especially in the cases of death and bodily injury.[15] There are more serious objections to including imprisonment among a list of paradigmatic harms. I shall deal with each of the paradigm cases in turn. There is something vaguely paradoxical in characterizing death as such as a harm. For one thing death is something that comes to us all, and, though 'the life everlasting' may be an attractive prospect in its religious meaning, more mundanely it is likely to evoke what Bernard Williams has aptly called 'the tedium of immortality'.[16] The grim reaper harvests us all eventually and if death is an evil it is not one which, *pace* Lucas, can be avoided. It may be objected, with some justification, that this is an absurdly literal rendering of Lucas's claim. By death he surely means, as is indicated by his later use of the expression 'being killed', death at another's hand. But is death at another's hand necessarily harmful to the person killed? There is perhaps here little room for disagreement except at the margins, but such margins do exist. It is surely not unintelligible for the perpetrator of an horrific crime, perhaps tortured by remorse and guilt, to see capital punishment as a blessing rather than a harm. Also the very sick or disabled may perceive their death as a release and the prolongation of their life as cruel and harmful.[17] Certainly this seems to have been Kafka's view shortly before his death in demanding of his friend, Klopstock, 'Kill me, or you're a murderer.'[18] Further, though more ambiguously, there have been Christian traditions in which life, 'a vale of tears', is at best a mixed blessing and in which a 'righteous' death is something to be striven for. What is incontestable, however, is that some kinds of death must be viewed as harmful from any moral perspective and in so far as this is true there is warrant for Lucas's claim. Even in the case of death though, as I have tried to show, there is some room for genuine disagreement about the kinds of death that may be thought harmful. There are circumstances within which even death at the hands of another may not be considered harmful either to the person killed or to others.

The claim that bodily injury is a paradigm case of something harmful is at least free from that tinge of paradox which is associated with Lucas's similar claim about death. Additionally it should be noted that just as 'death' seemed to mean 'being killed' in Lucas's argument, so 'bodily injury' becomes 'mutilation'. Here, however, it is immediately possible to see room for disagreement about what is to count as mutilation. For example, while male circumcision may be too trivial a matter to be regarded as 'mutilation' by anyone, what of so-called 'female circumcision' widely practised in Islamic cultures and allegedly not unknown among devout Muslims in this country? No doubt most non-Muslims would answer that it is mutilation but it is clear that many of the women concerned do not regard themselves as having been mutilated. Indeed some would regard it as harmful not to undergo such treatment and this response is quite intelligible in the context of Islamic conceptions of female sexuality. Nor are such ideas utterly unfamiliar to the Christian tradition. For example, there is a long history of Christian sects in which castration has been a norm or ideal for men.[19] According to Matthew, Christ tells us 'if thy eye offend thee, pluck it out, and cast it from thee: it is better to enter life with one eye, rather than having two eyes to be cast into hell fire'.[20] This need not be interpreted metaphorically.[21] Certainly such views are uncommon in our own society but there is no reason to think that we are bound not to take them seriously, as Lucas suggests. In any ethic in which penance plays a significant role, physical suffering may be one form which it takes, and, when understood in terms of penance, such suffering may not be seen as harmful at all. In short it is misleading to say, as does Lucas, that mutilation is a paradigm case of harm for though there may be general agreement that 'mutilation' is harmful, this may obscure serious and deep disagreements about what is to count as mutilation. There will be limits to such disagreement, but the important point for my argument is that they may be much broader than is readily appreciated.

Lucas's final paradigm of harm is that of imprisonment. Imprisonment is often part of a system of legal justice and it is in this context that I wish to consider it. Most people would probably agree with Lucas that in punishing criminals by imprisoning them we do them harm, and there is perhaps no alternative interpretation of the way penal institutions in our society actually work. Simone Weil, who also envisaged a very different possibility, certainly thought so:

> We have lost all idea of what punishment is. We are not aware that its purpose is to procure good for a man. For us it stops short with the infliction of harm. That is why there is one, and only one, thing in modern society more hideous than crime – namely repressive justice.[22]

This conception of punishment embodied in modern society is counterposed to a very different view:

> Punishment is a vital need of the human soul ... the most indispensable punishment for the soul is that inflicted for crime. By committing crime, a man places himself, of his own accord, outside the chain of eternal obligations which bind every human being to every other one. Punishment alone can weld him back again, fully so, if accompanied by consent on his part; otherwise only partially so. Just as the only way of showing respect for somebody suffering from hunger is to give him something to eat, so the only way of showing respect for somebody who has placed himself outside the law is to reinstate him inside the law by subjecting him to the punishment ordained by the law.[23]

In Weil's view, and something like it seems to go back at least as far as Plato's *Gorgias*, punishment is related to atonement, remorse and human community, and, when seen in this context, imprisonment may become not an obvious and undesirable harm but 'a vital need of the human soul'.

A similar conception of punishment seems to inform Sonia's response to Raskolnikov in *Crime and Punishment*. It is difficult to see how anyone holding the view of imprisonment espoused by Lucas could even begin to make sense of Sonia's actions and yet they are far from incomprehensible in the context of Dostoyevsky's story. It is clear that Sonia in urging Raskolnikov to confess and accept his punishment (which would be imprisonment) cannot be understood as wishing to harm him. If that were her motivation she could easily have informed on him herself. Yet she does not, and her whole attitude is one of love and concern for Raskolnikov's well-being. What she wants is for Raskolnikov to desire imprisonment for himself.

> 'Get up!' She seized him by the shoulder, and he raised himself, looking at her in astonishment. 'Go, at once this very minute, and stand at the crossroads, bow down, first kiss the earth which you have defiled, and then bow down to all the four corners of the world – and say to all men aloud, I am a murderer! Then God will send you life again. Will you go? Will you?' she asked him, trembling all over, seizing his hands and clasping them tightly in hers and looking at him with burning eyes.
>
> He was struck with amazement at the girl's sudden exaltation.
>
> 'Is it penal servitude you're thinking of, Sonia? Do you want me to give myself up?' he asked gloomily.
>
> 'Accept suffering, and be redeemed by it – that's what you must do.'[24]

If Lucas is right, we *must* think that Raskolnikov's response is the only possible one since, if he were persuaded by Sonia to want imprisonment for himself, we could not take him seriously. But the 'must' implied by Lucas is illusory for there is no necessity here. Indeed one does not even need to share Sonia's religious beliefs to feel the force of her appeal. Furthermore, Raskolnikov's spiritual rebirth and regeneration after his confession is shown to be not only the issue of Sonia's love but to grow out of the experience

122

of imprisonment itself, and there is nothing impossible or unintelligible in what Dostoyevsky depicts. In short, from the
perspectives of Sonia and Simone Weil, when part of a just system
of punishment, imprisonment, far from being a paradigm case of
harm, is positively beneficial.

So far, the argument has been that even the harms that Lucas
claims are paradigm cases are much more controversial than they
may appear. What kinds of death and which bodily trans-
formations are harmful are matters over which there is
considerable disagreement. In the case of imprisonment the scope
for disagreement is very wide indeed. However, even supposing
that there is agreement over what is harmful, it does not follow
that such agreement will extend to the degree or seriousness of the
harm involved. Even the so-called paradigm cases need not be
thought the worst of harms. This point is sufficiently obvious as
not to need detailed development. One example is provided by a
recent pronouncement by Mrs Thatcher in which she reveals that
while no doubt regarding her own death as something harmful she
apparently believes it would be a lesser harm than being subject
to a communist regime. This is a belief the consequences of which
she seems quite willing to inflict on the rest of us should the
occasion arise.[25] 'Better dead than red' may be a crude embodi-
ment of the view that there are worse things than death, but it is
a current view and it reminds us that there are a great many moral
perspectives from which though death may be seen as a harm, it
is far from being seen as the worst harm that may befall a person.
Every military ethic incorporates such a belief and the very idea
of 'death before dishonour' is hardly an uncommon one in moral
thought, despite much modern cynicism. A similar argument
could be developed concerning the relative weights attached to
bodily injury and imprisonment though I shall not do so. Thus,
even when the paradigm cases are agreed to be harmful, there is
frequent disagreement about the seriousness of such harms relative
to other non-paradigmatic harms and, in the light of this, the
paradigmatic status of Lucas's harms is distinctly odd. For, even
where the supposed paradigm cases are agreed to be harmful, some
people will view as still more serious harms conditions that others
do not see as harms at all.

The final point to be made about Lucas's paradigmatic harms

is closely connected to the previous one and concerns the undue emphasis that is given to material harms. Both death and bodily injury relate exclusively to physical well-being and, though imprisonment is more problematic to identify as exclusively material, it too is very physically oriented. In this Lucas shares, to some extent at least, a tendency prevalent in our times to think that material deprivations are always the most serious of harms, perhaps even the only 'real' harms. Again, however, such a view is far from uncontroversial. There is more cogency than is sometimes allowed, despite its complacency, in Carlyle's claim that:

> It is not what a man outwardly has or wants that constitutes the happiness or misery of him. Nakedness, hunger, distress of all kinds, death itself have been cheerfully suffered when the heart was right. It is the feeling of injustice that is insupportable to all men.[26]

This view receives some support from a person whose credentials to speak of the extremely poor in the contemporary world cannot be denied. Mother Teresa said of the poor of Calcutta that:

> It is not very often things they need. What they need much more is what we offer them. In these twenty years of work among the people, I have come more and more to realize that it is being unwanted that is the worst disease that any human being can ever experience.[27]

I mention these views not to diminish the significance or reality of physical and material suffering, nor to lend support to any cosy or convenient view about the dignity of poverty, but as a necessary corrective to an excessive emphasis on exclusively material harms. On almost any view of what is a worthwhile life there will be values, other than mere physical survival or good health, that make life worth living. Any threat to such values may be perceived to be quite as harmful as a threat to life itself. Of course what these values are may be subject to fierce and passionate dispute. In this respect, concentrating on material harms, where disagreement is likely to be less though not completely absent, is potentially misleading. In so far as the expression 'paradigm cases' suggests typicality, such material harms are perhaps rather atypical in the degree of consensus they inspire and this is a point which, as mentioned earlier, Lucas himself recognizes. It is nevertheless a point worth emphasizing.

The purpose of the argument so far has been to explore the limits of one approach which tries to establish an uncontroversial core of what is harmful. Although the argument has not shown that there is no such core, it has shown that if there is such a core it will at best form a small part of broader and more controversial conceptions of harm. While any such core will be far too narrowly circumscribed to do the work that Mill and other liberals characteristically require of the concept of harm, any richer conception is likely to be controversial as between different moral points of view. However Lucas's remark that 'to be harmful, a thing must be something that most people do not want' might be pursued more systematically than Lucas does. For rather than merely enumerate several things commonly regarded as harmful, it might be thought possible through the notion of wants to develop a conception of harm which is rooted in the 'analysis of the notion of harm itself'. This is the strategy adopted by R. M. Hare in his paper 'Wrongness and harm'.[28]

Hare's argument proceeds through an analysis of harm in terms of the infringement of interests and the infringement of interests in terms of the frustration of desires. For Hare 'to harm somebody is to act against his interests' and 'the notion of interests is tied in some way or other to the notion of desires and that of wanting'.[29] The nature of the connection between 'interests' and 'desires' and 'wanting' seems to be conceptual for:

> it would scarcely be intelligible to claim that a certain thing was in a man's interest, although he neither wanted it, nor had ever wanted it, nor would ever want it, nor anything that it was a necessary or sufficient means to.[30]

Thus for Hare the nature of the connection between wanting, interests and harms is such that:

> To speak very crudely and inexactly, to say that some act would harm somebody is to say that it would prevent some interests of his being satisfied, and this, in turn, is to say that it would, or might in possible circumstances, prevent some desire of his being realised.[31]

Hare regards this formulation as crude and inexact because if 'might' in the above quotation is taken to mean mere logical possibility then almost any act can be called harmful, and it is hard to see how 'might' can be restricted to give the formulation any specific content. This is a serious problem for Hare if he is to succeed in his attempt to circumscribe a plausible conception of what is harmful but it is not the only problem. In addition there are serious difficulties involved in Hare's attempt to connect 'interests' with 'wants' or 'desires' and I shall explore some of these in a moment.

The essence of Hare's view is that something is harmful to a person when it prevents some desire of that person from being realized. There are, as we have seen, two stages to the argument both of which involve conceptual claims. The first asserts that we cannot understand anything as harmful to a person unless we see it as an infringement of the interests, or destructive of the well-being, of that person. This claim seems to be correct and it is certainly not undermined by any of my earlier arguments. For example, the reason Simone Weil and Dostoyevsky are able to argue intelligibly that punishment is not harmful is precisely because they do not see it as infringing the interests of a person justly punished. If they had not succeeded in making such a claim intelligible we would surely have been unable to understand their claims as arguments about what is harmful. The second stage of Hare's argument, which asserts a connection between interests and 'wants' or 'desires' (or in his more technical term 'prescriptions'), is more obscure and problematic. Hare concedes that 'it is not universally the case that if we want something, it is in our own interest to have it, nor that if something is in our interest we want it.' He believes these connections between interests and wants are too crude. Hare repeats his own earlier account in *Freedom and Reason*, when he claims that 'to have an interest is for there to be something which one wants (or may want), or which is (or may be) a means, necessary or sufficient for the attainment of something which one wants (or may want).'[32] In his more recent work Hare has claimed that the 'desires' related to interests in the way he describes are rational or prudential desires. He writes:

whether I am prescribing in my own interest or in someone

126

else's ... I must ask, not what I or he does actually at present wish, but what prudentially speaking, we should wish. It is from this rational point of view (in the prudential sense of 'rational') that I have to give my universal prescriptions.[33]

Thus the desires which are connected to interests are what would be desired if we were perfectly prudent; that is 'fully informed and unconfused'.[34] Interests therefore are tied conceptually to 'rational' desires rather than the desires which people may happen to have. To harm a person then is to frustrate the satisfaction of their 'rational' desires.

It is fairly obvious why Hare is driven to qualify the connection between interests and desires in this way. For if the connection were merely between interests and the actual desires a person happens to have at a particular time, it would lead to some odd consequences. For example, we would be logically obliged to say of the drug addict that providing him with plentiful supplies of the drug he wants was acting in his interest while preventing him access to such a supply, even while encouraging and aiding the addict to seek treatment, would be harming him. However, it is far from clear that the notion of prudential rationality, especially in the absence of any developed theory of prudence, solves Hare's problems. Indeed it potentially introduces an extra one for, depending upon how prudential rationality is to be understood, it might seriously compromise Hare's professed liberalism. As Sparshott has observed, 'As soon as a person's "interests" are allowed to extend more widely than his actual present desires the door is wide open to do-gooders of all kinds.'[35] Though Hare's own drawing of the line against such interference is suitably liberal, it does not seem to be guided by any considerations other than his own liberal preferences about where such a line should be drawn.[36] While we may or may not share these preferences there is certainly nothing compelling about them as mere preferences.

If Hare were correct in holding that there is a conceptual connection between what a person 'rationally' wants and what is in that person's interest, it would follow that judgements about whether something was harmful to somebody, though relative to that person's desires, would be, in principle at least, uncontroversial. It would be a matter of fact whether a person desired something and it would be a further fact whether something else prevented the realization of that desire. If it did, it would be harmful; if it did not, it would be harmless. However the most powerful objection to this account of harm is that the conceptual connection which is alleged to hold between interests and 'rational desires' is simply untenable in the form Hare presents it. The logic of 'interests' is crucially different from that of 'wants' or 'desires', such that we can and frequently do contrast them. Nor is this contrast entirely explicable in terms of any conception of prudential rationality which would not be merely stipulative. What a person desires may or may not be in his or her interest, and what is in a person's interest may not be what he or she desires even when he or she is 'fully informed and unconfused'. For example, on Hare's view, it would be unintelligible to say of a man who has a strong desire to read pornographic magazines, assuming he is fully aware of the consequences, that satisfying this desire would be harmful to him. However, whether or not one agrees with such a claim, it is surely not unintelligible. The problem is that Hare cannot allow that it makes sense to see any desires themselves as potentially harmful to the person whose desires they are, unless such desires can be shown to be lacking in prudence. Yet if moral corruption is intelligibly to be thought of as a serious harm that might befall a person, then Hare's account of the relationship between desires and interests, and *a fortiori* his conception of harm, are unsatisfactory.[37]

It may be that in one respect the above argument is too quick. For it has been claimed, by Joel Feinberg for example, that moral corruption only harms a person if that person has a desire to be virtuous.[38] Hare's remarks about the amoralist suggest he would agree. Feinberg too is concerned to defend an entirely 'want-regarding' conception of interest and this leads him to conclude that:

> Morally corrupting a person, that is causing him to be a worse person than he would otherwise be, can *harm* him, therefore, only if he has an antecedent interest in being good. (It may in fact harm no one to corrupt him if he is corrupted in a way that does not make him dangerous to others.) The moral corruption or neglect of an unformed child, then, is no direct harm to him,

provided that he has the resources to pursue his own interests effectively anyway, but it can be a very real harm to his parents if *they* have a powerful stake in the child's moral development.[39]

Though Feinberg reveals himself to be admirably clear-headed about the implication of his view, as is shown in the second part of the quotation, there is surely something very odd in claiming that morally corrupting young children, though possibly harmful to the parents, in no way harms the child. Such a restricted conception of interests seems simply a misrepresentation. In part at least, this results from Feinberg's conception of a morality as something optional: as if it were like an interest in opera that we might or might not have. What is mistaken about this view is shown in some comments of Wittgenstein who remarks:

> Supposing that I could play tennis and one of you saw me playing and said 'Well you play pretty badly' and suppose I answered 'I know, I'm playing badly but I don't want to play any better,' all the other man could say would be 'Ah then that's all right.' But suppose I had told one of you a preposterous lie and he came up to me and said 'You're behaving like a beast' and then I were to say 'I know I behave badly, but then I don't want to behave any better,' could he then say 'Ah, then that's all right'? Certainly not; he would say 'Well you *ought* to want to behave better.'[40]

Characteristically, morality is not conceived as something which is merely optional, to be taken up or not like tennis according to the tastes and preferences of the individual. Whether a morality must be conceived of in this way is not a matter which can be entered into here but for my purposes the weaker claim, that a morality may be and often is viewed as compelling in the way Wittgenstein describes, is sufficient. For if a morality is understood in this manner, then from the point of view of that morality, to act morally will be in a person's best interests and moral corruption will necessarily be thought harmful, whether or not this is recognized by the person morally corrupted. In short, there is no compelling reason why the judgement of the person morally corrupted must be decisive in determining whether the person is harmed: that the individual denies that he or she is harmed may indeed be seen as an indication of the extent to which the individual has been corrupted.

The purpose of the discussion so far has been to undermine in a general way the view that what is considered harmful is largely independent of or shared by competing moral perspectives. Though there has been no attempt to consider all the strategies by which such a view might be defended, the approaches of Lucas and Hare, or some variation on them, seem to be among the most plausible and popular.[41] Neither of these approaches, it has been argued, is capable of generating a sufficiently substantial and un-controversial conception of harm to fulfil the function required of the concept of harm in liberal theory. For what is regarded as harmful is itself in part constituted by particular moral conceptions; consequently the concept of harm is largely a blunt instrument for resolving the practical question of whether some activity should be tolerated where the moral quality of that activity is a matter of a dispute. The view that such a question can be resolved by putting to one side the moral differences which divide the parties to such a dispute and focusing on the question of whether the activity is harmful, as if the moral differences and conceptions of harm had no connection, reveals a deep mis-understanding of the concept of harm. Furthermore, this can be seen not only at the rather general level at which most of the discussion so far has been conducted but also in relation to very specific practical questions such as those concerning the toleration of pornography, various kinds of sexual practice, blasphemy, different religious practices and similar issues. In order to bring out the general point in a specific context I shall give a very brief consideration to the question of whether pornography is harmful.

In considering the question of the alleged harmfulness of pornography it is necessary to introduce a distinction between private or individual harms, on the one hand, and public or social harms on the other. This is necessary because the harms at issue are often social or public harms rather than direct harms to other individuals. A public or social harm is understood as something that is harmful to others through its damaging the physical environment, culture or morality of a community. Many of the arguments which claim that tolerating pornography is harmful, even to those who do not directly encounter it, rely on a conception of public or social harms. This came across clearly to the Committee on Obscenity and Film Censorship. In their Report they write:

> The broadest arguments put to us concerned the social harms flowing from the widespread availability of pornography, in terms of cultural pollution, moral deterioration and the undermining of human compassion, social values and basic institutions. Arguments of this kind were less concerned with the possibility of specific effects on individual behaviour than with the gradual infecting of society with a disregard for decency, or lack of respect for others, a taste for the base, or contempt for restraint and responsibility: in short with the weakening of our civilisation and the demoralisation of society.[42]

The Committee take seriously some of these arguments but they consistently interpret them as causal claims. The question they ask is what evidence there is that pornography is a cause of these harms (i.e. is harmful through its contingent effects). The main burden of the conclusions is that pornography is a symptom rather than a cause of this moral decline (if such it be), but they never seriously confront the possibility that these arguments against pornography are open to a different interpretation. On this alternative interpretation the argument in terms of social harm is not concerned to establish a causal relationship between pornography and the social harms described because, from the moral perspective which informs this argument, pornography is in part constitutive of these harms. There is no empirical enquiry necessary to show that pornography is harmful on this interpretation since the harm of pornography lies in its nature and not its effects.[43] It is not a contingent question whether or not pornography is harmful for it is part of the very meaning of pornography that from this moral perspective it cannot but be seen as harmful.[44] Of course this is not to deny that there are other moral perspectives from which the issue of whether or not pornography is harmful *will* be seen as a contingent or empirical question requiring suitable research to be answered. What this suggests is that the concept of harm as such provides no Archimedean point from which we can judge whether or not pornography should be legally tolerated. And this is so even though the parties to the dispute may agree that the harmfulness of pornography is a morally necessary condition for its prohibition. Where the parties will not agree is over what they regard as the harms involved and similar disagreements are at the root of many other disputes about whether or not some activity should be tolerated.

It has not been the intention of this essay to offer a comprehensive discussion of harm or even a thorough account of the relationship between harm and morality. Both tasks are too large for this short essay. Rather the concern has been to consider the plausibility of the view, often associated with liberalism, that harm, or harm to others, can provide a practically useful criterion for resolving most disputes about whether or not some activity should be tolerated. The conclusion of the argument is that this view is largely implausible. However, it should also be made clear that it is not part of the argument developed here to claim that because an activity may be conceived as harmful from a particular moral perspective this is a sufficient reason for its being prohibited. When the question of legislation arises, it will often be necessary to prohibit what some see as harmless though others do not, and permit what some see as harmful though others disagree. In any community in which there are significant differences in moral viewpoint there will be no alternative to this. However, in so far as liberalism purports to maintain some kind of neutrality between different moral perspectives it fails to recognize this and attempts the impossible.[45] What liberalism represents as the neutral requirement of preventing harm to others will be perceived by those with different conceptions of what is harmful as the enforcement of a morality they do not share. Liberalism itself embodies substantial moral precepts and ideals and its conception of what is harmful has no self-evidently greater claim to primacy than that of other moral viewpoints. For there may be no rationally compelling or objective way of resolving these differences. The philosopher, though he may have his sympathies, has no stone to unturn, and if the argument of this essay is broadly correct this should not occasion any surprise. Perhaps what is surprising is that anyone should think differently. Are we to believe that the real and deep moral differences that divide humanity will not be reflected in different con-

132

ceptions of what is harmful? If this is what the liberal believes then liberalism is in bad trouble.

Notes

I am most grateful for the very helpful written comments on an earlier draft of this essay to David Edwards, Susan Mendus, Peter Nicholson and Professor D. D. Raphael.

1 J. S. Mill, *On Liberty*, London, 1859. Edition quoted is that edited by G. Himmelfarb, Harmondsworth, 1974, 68.
2 C. L. Ten, *Mill On Liberty*, Oxford, 1980.
3 ibid., 62.
4 Ten's interpretation of Mill is criticized in T. Honderich, '"On Liberty" and morality-dependent harms', *Political Studies*, 30, 1982, and in J. Gray, *Mill On Liberty: A Defence*, Oxford, 1983.
5 e.g. D. R. Knowles, 'A reformulation of the harm principle', *Political Theory*, 6, 1978. Other problems associated with 'the harm principle' are discussed in C. Goodrum, 'Notes on the harm principle', *The Personalist*, 57, 1976, and in Peter Jones's contribution to this volume.
6 For a particularly impressive recent attempt see J. Gray, op. cit.
7 cf. D. Lyons, *Forms and Limits of Utilitarianism*, Oxford, 1965, and B. Williams's contribution to J. C. Smart and B. Williams, *Utilitarianism: For and Against*, London, 1973.
8 The 'liberal' as here characterized is a construct of my own. I do not mean to suggest that the two propositions attributed to the 'liberal' are either necessary or sufficient conditions for anyone to be properly described as a liberal. However, I do think that these two propositions, or some slight variation on them, are prominent in liberal political thought.
9 A broadly similar case is argued in D. Z. Phillips and H. O. Mounce, *Moral Practices*, London, 1969.
10 *Guardian*, 29 March 1983.
11 *Guardian*, 21 April 1983.
12 B. Williams (ed.), *Obscenity and Film Censorship*, Cambridge, 1981, 50.
13 J. R. Lucas, *The Principles of Politics*, Oxford, 1966, 172.
14 ibid., 173.

15 Although no attempt is made in this essay to establish precisely what these limits might be, that there may be such limits is not denied.

16 'The Makropulos Case: reflections on the tedium of immortality', in B. Williams, *Problems of the Self*, London, 1973.

17 A recent example is Elizabeth Bouvia, a severely handicapped American, who tried to establish a legal right to die.

18 As reported in M. Brod, *Franz Kafka: A Biography*, New York, 1960, 212, and R. Hayman, *Kafka*, London, 1981, 303.

19 For a history of such sects in Russia see F. C. Conybeare, *Russian Dissenters*, Cambridge, Mass., 1921.

20 Matthew 18: 9.

21 cf. the account of Brentano's attitude to his blindness in D. Z. Phillips and H. O. Mounce, op. cit., 57–8.

22 'Human personality', in S. Weil, *Selected Essays 1934–43*, trans. and ed. R. Rees, London, 1962, 31.

23 S. Weil, *The Need for Roots*, trans. A. F. Willis, London, 1952, 20. For a profound exploration of some aspects of this view of punishment see P. Winch's essays, 'Can a good man be harmed?' and 'Ethical reward and punishment', both reprinted in P. Winch, *Ethics and Action*, London, 1972.

24 F. Dostoyevsky, *Crime and Punishment*, trans. D. Magarshak, Harmondsworth, 1951, 433–4.

25 These views are inferred from reports of a press conference given by Mrs Thatcher in spring 1983.

26 'Chartism', in *Thomas Carlyle: Selected Writings*, ed. A. Shelston, Harmondsworth, 1971, 177.

27 Quoted in C. MacMillan, *Women, Reason and Nature*, Oxford, 1982, 22.

28 'Wrongness and Harm', in R. M. Hare, *Essays on the Moral Concepts*, London, 1972.

29 ibid., 97.

30 ibid., 98.

31 ibid.

32 ibid., 97.

33 R. M. Hare, 'Ethical theory and Utilitarianism', in H. D. Lewis (ed.), *Contemporary British Philosophy*, 4th series, London, 1976, 119.

34 ibid.

35 F. Sparshott, 'Critical study of "Freedom and Reason"', *Philosophical Quarterly*, 14, 1964.

36 Of course not all Utilitarians have been liberals, as is evidenced by Mill's contemporary, J. F. Stephen, *Liberty, Equality and Fraternity*, London, 1967.

37 Hare sometimes distinguishes sharply between 'ideals' and 'interests' but this distinction seems to play no role in his argument in 'Wrongness and harm', op. cit. For some important criticisms of that distinction and the use Hare makes of it, see R. N. Berki, 'Interests and moral ideals', *Philosophy*, 49, 1974.

38 J. Feinberg, 'Harm and self-interest', in P. Hacker and J. Raz (eds), *Law, Morality and Society*, Oxford, 1977.

39 ibid., 290.

40 'Wittgenstein's lecture on ethics', *Philosophical Review*, 74, 1965, 5.

41 See also J. Kleinig, 'Crime and the concept of harm', *American Philosophical Quarterly*, 15, 1978.

42 B. Williams (ed.), *Obscenity*, op. cit., 92.

43 One member of the Williams Committee has rather grudgingly recognized the seriousness of this issue and the limitations of the Report's treatment of it. See A. W. B. Simpson, *Pornography and Politics*, London, 1983, 79–80.

44 This line of thought about pornography is explored in much greater depth in the contribution to this volume by Susan Mendus.

45 The argument of this essay attacks the claim of liberalism to moral neutrality only as this is related to the concept of harm. For two defences of how liberalism can be neutral, see B. A. Ackerman, *Social Justice in the Liberal State*, New Haven, 1980, and R. Dworkin, 'Liberalism', in S. Hampshire (ed.), *Public and Private Morality*, Cambridge, 1978.

7

Toleration, harm and moral effect

PETER JONES

How are we to set the limits of toleration? John Stuart Mill's answer is well known and has been endorsed by many another advocate of toleration:

> the only purpose for which power can be rightfully exercised over any member of a civilised community, against his will, is to prevent harm to others. His own good, either physical or moral, is not a sufficient warrant. He cannot rightfully be compelled to do or forbear because it will be better for him to do so, because it will make him happier, because, in the opinion of others, to do so would be wise, or even right.[1]

For Mill, that an action 'harmed' another was not of itself conclusive proof that it ought not to be tolerated. Its harmfulness merely established that it was eligible for restriction.

> As soon as any part of a person's conduct affects prejudicially the interests of others, society has jurisdiction over it, and the question whether the general welfare will or will not be promoted by interfering with it, becomes open to discussion.[2]

Thus, if we follow Mill, we should ask two questions in deciding whether an action should be tolerated:

1   Does it harm others?
2   If so, is that harm, all things considered, such as to justify not tolerating the action?

The second question warns us not to expect an easy answer. There may be a great many things to be considered and people may differ over what they believe to be relevant considerations and over the relative importance that should be given to each. By contrast, the first question looks relatively simple. After all it asks no more than whether an action should be subject to the second question. However, anyone who has the merest acquaintance with this subject knows that that simplicity is deceptive. Mill's own rather ambiguous remarks in *On Liberty* have caused much dispute amongst his interpreters over the meaning he intended to give to 'harm'. Is an action removed from the self-regarding category if it 'affects' others or only if it affects their 'interests'? If the latter, how are we to define a person's interests? How are we to understand Mill's own distinctions between 'direct effects' upon others, which fall within the compass of the harm principle, and 'indirect effects' which do not? Does Mill equate harm with the violation of rights or the non-performance of duties or neither? Do I harm someone only if I injure them or can I harm by failing to benefit?

One particularly difficult area of controversy is that examined by John Horton is this volume. Is harm a notion which, although it may figure in moral judgements, is not itself a moral notion, or are moral judgements already present in what we consider to be harmful? How, for instance, are we to categorize the distress caused to people by the actions of others but which arises only because they believe those actions to be morally wrong? Can we say that a person's character has been corrupted or worsened without resorting to moral criteria? Can we decide how the harm principle relates to a subject such as abortion without pre-judging the issue morally? As Horton shows, even imprisonment, physical injury and death are not uncontroversially value-free harms.

In this essay I want to examine an argument which incorporates morality in the harm principle but in a way quite different from the cases that I have just instanced. The argument runs as follows. A wishes to do x which, it is believed, will result, or is likely to result, in his being in condition y. If A were in condition y, B would have a duty to assist him. The performance of that duty would be onerous for B. B may therefore prevent A from doing x, not for A's own good, but to protect B himself from incurring a burdensome duty.

137

Thus take Mill's famous example of the unsafe bridge.[3] If B sees A about to cross a bridge which B knows to be unsafe, and B has no time to warn A of the danger, then, according to Mill, B may justifiably 'seize' A and turn him back; 'for liberty consists in doing what one desires' and, under the circumstances, B can reasonably presume that A does not wish to risk falling in the river. However, if B has time to warn A of the risks, it is then entirely up to A whether he incurs them and B has no right forcibly to restrain A. So far so good. But let's insert an additional ingredient into Mill's example. Suppose that, if A were to fall into the river, B would be duty-bound to jump in and rescue him. The existence of such a duty would quite alter the picture. B could then claim that, in crossing the unsafe bridge, A was imposing risks not only upon himself but also upon B – the risk that B will have to undergo the inconvenience and possible hazards of rescuing A. A's act is no longer self-regarding; B's interests are also at stake and, in the name of those interests, he may claim a right to prevent A from crossing the bridge.

Henceforth I shall call this the 'moral effect argument'. The sort of example I have just given involves the simple relation between individuals that is often described as requiring 'Good Samaritanism'. However, the moral effect argument is not confined to one-to-one acts of assistance and is more frequently, and perhaps more importantly, encountered in relation to collective provision against individual mishaps. In this context the argument takes the form that a society is justified in prohibiting certain sorts of conduct, or in compelling individuals to provide against certain risks, since, otherwise, the costs of those actions will have to be borne by the society. Thus those who argue for the legal prohibition of smoking often deny that they are motivated by a desire to save tobacco-smokers from themselves. Rather, they say, they are simply seeking to prevent careless individuals inflicting unnecessary medical costs upon the rest of society. The same sort of argument is often used in defence of compulsory seat belt and motorcycle helmet legislation. When it is reasonably within its capability to save life or treat injury, a society has no moral option but to do so. But, if it cannot escape those moral obligations, a society can at least take steps to prevent careless individuals adding to them unnecessarily.

138

The moral effect argument has some notable liberal exponents. Consider the following passage from Hayek's *Constitution of Liberty*.[4]

> Once it becomes the recognized duty of the public to provide for the extreme needs of old age, unemployment, sickness, etc., irrespective of whether the individuals could and ought to have made provision themselves, ... it seems an obvious corollary to compel them to insure (or to otherwise provide) against those common hazards of life. The justification in this case is not that people should be coerced to do what is in their individual interest but that, by neglecting to make provision, they would become a charge to the public. Similarly, we require motorists to insure against third-party risks, not in their interest but in the interest of others who might be harmed by their action.

A similar argument is cited by Milton Friedman in relation to old-age pensions.[5]

> A possible justification on liberal principles for compulsory purchase of annuities is that the improvident will not suffer the consequence of their own action but will impose costs on others. We shall not, it is said, be willing to see the indigent aged suffer in dire poverty. We shall assist them by private and public charity. Hence the man who does not provide for his old age will become a public charge. Compelling him to buy an annuity is justified not for his own good but for the good of the rest of us.

Unlike Hayek, Friedman does not find this an adequate justification for compelling people to provide for their old age. However, his rejection of the argument stems from what he believes to be the 'facts' – that, in the absence of compulsion, the great majority of the population would still provide for their old age and only a tolerable minority would become a public charge. Significantly, he finds nothing improper in the appeal to moral effect itself.

★

Before I subject the moral effect argument to examination, let me note some features of the argument itself. For many the appeal of the argument is that it conforms to the spirit of Mill's harm principle. It provides an other-regarding justification for measures which, at first blush, might seem to admit of only paternalistic justification. However, the argument is obviously not a straightforward application of the harm principle. Hayek's attempt to present the public charge argument as really no different from the argument for requiring motorists to insure against third-party risks is quite misleading. If I drive a car I impose a risk of personal injury or damage to property upon others and, ordinarily, there is nothing problematic about identifying those as harms. If I fail to provide for my ill-health and fall sick then, setting aside effects on dependants or the possibility that I may become a danger to the health of others (considerations which do not figure in the moral effect argument), I do not inflict harm upon anyone in the same sense. I 'invade the interests' of others only granted the assumption that they have the duty to assist me. If we do not grant that assumption, there is no harmful effect upon others and the case for compelling me to provide for my ill-health disappears. The presumption of a duty to assist is therefore pivotal in the moral effect argument.

Nor is it enough that that duty be an established legal duty. If there were such a legal duty and we had to treat it as an unalterable social fact, the public charge argument would not be so very different from the argument for compelling motorists to insure against third-party risks. But if we are subjecting social institutions themselves to examination, we have to ask why there should be such an established public duty. Why not have arrangements which allow people to do as they please, subject to the harm principle in its unmoralized form, and require them to suffer the full consequences of their own actions? The argument we are considering can meet that objection only by appeal to *moral* effects, that is, by asserting the moral rather than the merely legal duty to assist others in distress.

The argument must also hold that the moral duty really is a 'duty' and therefore morally inescapable. It would not be enough to regard B's assisting A as meritorious but not obligatory, for it would hardly do to limit A's freedom simply to provide against the possibility that B might then choose to assist him. It is odd that

140

Friedman appeals to 'charity' in his statement of the moral effect argument.[6] Charity is usually conceived as a matter of super-erogation and therefore something which is at the discretion of the potential donor. It would be a strange liberal who argued for the restraint of A's conduct to prevent his becoming a possible object of the grace and favour of others. If the moral effect argument is to be at all convincing, the duty to which it appeals must be one of strict obligation rather than discretionary virtue.

Finally, let me dispose of what might appear to be a contra-diction within the moral effect argument. According to the argument, B is justified in preventing A from doing x to protect himself from being saddled with a burdensome duty. Now if B is justified in limiting A's freedom, that would seem to imply that A, in doing x, would be 'wronging' or 'harming' B. That is, A himself ought not to impose moral effects upon B. If that were not true, how could the limit upon A's freedom be justified? But if A does something which wrongs B, it seems odd to hold that the consequence of that should be that B owes a duty to A. How can B owe a duty to A as a result of a wrong done to B by A?

To pose this question is to make the moral effect argument appear paradoxical in a way that it is not. To begin with, it is by no means absurd to speak of B's having a duty to A as a con-sequence of A's failing in a duty to B. Take the case of seat belts. A may owe it to others, and not just to himself, to wear a seat belt because others will have to cope with the consequences if A suffers serious injury because of his neglect. When A fails to wear a seat belt, therefore, he is failing in a duty to B. But if he does 'wrong' B in this way and suffers serious injury, it does not seem odd to hold that B nevertheless has a duty to assist A rather than leave him bleeding at the roadside. Indeed the 'nevertheless' here is out of place because A can wrong B only if B has a duty to assist A in those circumstances. If B had no duty to come to the aid of those who failed to wear seat belts, A would not be wronging B in failing to wear a belt. Thus, although *temporally* B's duty to A follows upon A's wrong to B, *logically* it is the other way round. For A wrongs B only because and in so far as B has a duty to A. That is why it would be quite misleading to represent B's duty as a gratuitous return of good for evil.

★

The moral effect argument raises very large issues concerning the weight that we should give to individual liberty and the duties that we owe to one another. Those issues are too large and too substantive to enable one to demonstrate the acceptability or otherwise of the appeal to moral effect in all its possible varieties. Rather I shall confine myself to examining the legitimacy of the appeal to moral effect where that appeal occurs in the context of liberal argument – which is, after all, where it is most likely to occur. Should a proponent of toleration, who conceives himself as belonging to the same tradition as J. S. Mill, be happy to embrace the moral effect argument?

An obvious practical danger of allowing appeals to moral effect is that we shall find the list of alleged moral effects lengthening. All manner of human activities involve risks and, if people are allowed to invoke their duty to cope with the consequences as a reason for proscribing those activities, individual freedom will rapidly vanish. Invoke moral effect in the case of seat belts and you place yourself at the top of a slippery slope at the bottom of which lies a world in which the prevention of heart disease provides justification for compulsory long-distance runs and obligatory Japanese-style diets. Indeed, this may lie only half way down the slope. Who can tell where the proliferation of alleged duties, and the consequent restrictions upon freedom, will end? Much of the appeal of the harm principle would seem to depend upon its providing a reasonably precise, empirical criterion for determining when interference is justified and when it is not. The belief that it does may be unduly optimistic but, even if the notion of harm is soft at the edges, it may still be thought hard at its centre. However, if the notion of harm is made entirely dependent upon a conception of duty, as it is in the moral effect argument, it may seem to lose all agreed meaning. The principle becomes hopelessly controversial and its practical effect is to place the freedom of the individual entirely at the mercy of others' conception of their duty towards him. No longer can it be said that 'over himself, over his own body and mind, the individual is sovereign'.[7]

Moreover, the moral effect argument can be used to produce an oddly inverse relation between humanity and tolerance. The more humane a person, the greater the range of cases in which he will feel obliged to assist people in coping with the consequences of their own actions. But every such duty can then be used as justification for preventing those consequences arising. Thus the more generous one is about the duties one has to others, the more ungenerous one can be about the freedom that they should be allowed.

While these might be acknowledged as real dangers, they may not be thought enough to sink the moral effect argument. Good arguments, like good tools, may be used badly or wrongly but that does not oblige us to abandon them. All that the slippery slope objection shows is the need to limit the appeal to moral effect. Once a set of rights and duties has been justified and given precise definition, the slide towards intolerance ceases to be an objection – at least in theory. However, in addition to its practical dangers, the appeal to moral effect confronts the liberal with more formal difficulties.

Let me restate the moral effect argument by listing the claims that it entails.

    (i)   A wishes to engage in conduct x which will, or is likely to, result in his being in condition y.
    (ii)   B has a duty to assist those in condition y.
    (iii) The performance of that duty would be onerous for B.
    (iv) The onerous character of that duty is such as to justify A's being prevented from doing x.

I shall consider these in reverse order.

Claim (iv) is phrased more cautiously than I have stated the concluding claims of the moral effect argument hitherto. However, it needs to be stated in that way to avoid pre-judging the issue of how the duty of B should weigh against the freedom of A. It would be possible for someone to accept claims (i), (ii) and (iii) but not to accept the restriction of A's freedom because, in the particular case in question, claim (iv) had not been met. There may be reasons for giving an absolute weight to A's freedom or to B's duty but, if not, an assessment of claim (iv) will have to wait upon the circumstances of each particular case. However, the indeterminate character of claim (iv) need not stand in the way of a general assessment of the moral effect argument. Earlier I noted that, for Mill, the harm principle defined what was eligible for restriction rather than what ought to be restricted. Similarly, we may regard moral effect as a criterion of what it is permissible to restrict rather than a criterion of what ought always to be restricted. In other words, we can examine whether the appeal to moral effect constitutes a legitimate reason for limiting freedom while accepting that, even if it does, it may not always constitute a conclusive reason.

Claim (iii) is that B's duty is onerous. That may seem to involve an unduly 'protestant' conception of duty. Moreover, if we were to restate claim (iii) in terms of Mill's harm principle (as, presumably, we should be able to) we would have to say that the imposition of that duty 'harmed' B which may seem a rather forced use of language. Nevertheless, if such a duty could be imposed by A upon B, it would certainly fall within the compass that Mill intended to give the harm principle. Most interpreters are agreed that 'harm' can be analysed in terms of interests and, on virtually any analysis of B's interests, those would be affected by his incurring a duty.

Of course (iii) involves the claim not only that B's interests are affected but that they are *adversely* affected and that may seem more open to argument. Might not the devout Christian welcome a proliferation of such duties as affording him yet more opportunities to manifest his love of God through service to mankind? However, I am concerned with moral effect in the context of liberal values and, for the liberal, whatever else might be said of B's duty, it has at least one undesirable feature which is that it restricts B's freedom. It is important to recall that we are considering neither a duty which is a permanent feature of the moral landscape, nor an obligation which B has himself assumed, but a duty which B has incurred without choice and which he would not have had but for the conduct of A.

I want to give rather closer attention to claims (i) and (ii) since I believe that it is here that the representation of the moral effect argument as a genuinely 'other-regarding' argument is open to question. The argument is clearly conceived by its users as avoiding any simple assertion that B cannot possibly allow A to inflict harm upon himself. A's conduct is to be restricted not for the good of A but for the good of B – to prevent B incurring a duty. But what is the nature of that duty? In the circumstances contemplated in the moral effect argument, B's duty must be conceived as a duty

144

to benefit A. Whether, in this sort of case, it would be appropriate to hold that A had a right in virtue of B's duty does not, I think, matter. What does matter is that the duty is a duty in respect of A and A is the intended beneficiary of that duty. There is no pretence in the moral effect argument that B's duty to assist A is really a duty to benefit third parties such as A's dependants or others to whom he has obligations. Thus B's duty in respect of A must entail a conception of what is good for A. That conception of A's good may not derive from B himself but may have been prescribed for B by others. But that makes no difference to the point at issue. Moreover, it is presumed in the moral effect argument that B's duty cannot be disposed of by A. If A were free to do x on the understanding that he thereby waived any duty of B to relieve him from the consequences, the issue of moral effect would not arise. It is because B is conceived as having a duty to relieve A from y, in spite of its being the consequence of A's freely choosing to do x, that B is thought justified in preventing A from encountering y. Thus A has no discretion over B's duty. Now if B's duty entails a conception of what is good for A and if A is unable to waive the duty, the moral effect argument entails imposing upon A a conception of what is for his good independent of, and quite possibly in opposition to, A's own conception of what is for his good.

To see this more clearly, let us review the ways in which A may take issue with B's claims. Firstly A may question the alleged undesirability of condition y. If this signals no more than that A and B have different preferences with respect to y, B's professed duty to relieve A from y is unsustainable. However the dispute is unlikely to be so simple. Those who oppose fluoridation, compulsory social security and prohibitions on high-risk activities do not usually express a preference for rotten teeth, poverty and death. An alternative focus of the dispute may be over what A's wishes would be were he actually to experience y. A believes that he would not find y undesirable or that he would not find y so undesirable that he could not possibly waive B's duty to relieve him. B believes otherwise. B's questioning of A's own estimate of his future wants is not entirely implausible. Since the wants in question are A's wants, A may seem to be placed in a unique position as far as any judgement about his future wants is concerned. However, that estimate involves a judgement about the nature of condition y as well as about the character of A's wants. B's view may rest upon his belief that A has an imperfect understanding of what condition y is really like. Does A really understand what it is like to experience withdrawal symptoms or to be racked by disease? However, even though B may have good grounds for questioning A's judgement about his future wants, the issue remains squarely one about what is good for A himself. This line of argument therefore does nothing to evade the objection that self-regarding reasons are being invoked to justify limitations upon A's freedom.

Secondly, A may agree that condition y would be undesirable but dispute B's claim that he would be duty-bound to relieve A from y. Indeed, A may prefer not to be relieved by B because he would rather suffer the consequences of his own actions than the humiliation of being saved from them by others. In that case the liberal must surely give A a veto over B's duty. To do otherwise would be not merely to allow but to require B to override A's conception of his own good. So far from holding that B had a duty to act in that way, the liberal typically would hold that that is precisely the sort of thing that B had a duty *not* to do.

A third source of dispute might be the relative merits of x and y. The moral effect argument results not only in A being spared consequence y, but also in his being prevented from doing x. Thus it pre-empts A's choice with respect to x + y rather than y alone. A proponent of moral effect cannot therefore rest his case merely upon the badness of y for A and the consequent duty of B with respect to A. He must also take account of x + y. If the good of x outweighs the bad of y, B can hardly make plausible his claim to embargo x + y. (Although, in these circumstances, it would seem equally implausible to ascribe a duty to B to cope with y.) But even if, on B's reckoning, the good of x is less than the bad of y, that cannot serve as an acceptable liberal reason for limiting A's conduct. That would be simply to allow B's judgement about the merits of x + y for A to supersede A's own judgement.

Finally, A and B may differ not over A's wants with respect to either x or y but over the purely technical matter of the connection between x and y. In other words, the dispute is really over the truth of claim (i). That dispute may not be a simple one. For example, it may be not about whether y will or will not be consequent upon x, but about the probability that y will be consequent upon x. A paternalistic intervention based upon the claim that someone is mistaken about the best way of satisfying his wants may be less objectionable than one resting upon a claim that he is mistaken about his wants. But it is a paternalistic intervention none the less and there is a well-rehearsed catalogue of liberal arguments for resisting it.

One such argument is that each individual is the best judge of his own interests. If that dictum were accepted, it would imply that A must be a better judge than B of the truth of claim (i) and, therefore, that B's assertion of (i) cannot be an adequate justification for his overriding A's wishes. The best-judge principle is difficult to take seriously as a simple exceptionless truth[8] and it often turns out to be an imprecise statement of one of two other positions. One of these is that an individual's wants relate not only to what he seeks to achieve but also to how he seeks to achieve it – so much so that each individual must be left to decide for himself how he pursues his ends. On this interpretation the best-judge principle reduces to the position that each must be the ultimate authority on his own wants. The other construction sometimes placed upon the principle is that it is good policy to act as if it were true.[9] If, as Mill held, when a society does interfere with an individual for his own good, 'the odds are that it interferes wrongly, and in the wrong place',[10] the best policy will be to act as if each individual were the best judge of his interests even though, on occasion, that may be untrue. However, neither of these reconstructions of the best-judge principle disturbs the conclusion that the truth of claim (i) is to be assessed by A rather than B.

However, many liberal arguments on this issue turn not upon the quality of each individual's judgement but upon the rightness or desirability of his being in command of his own life. Thus the claim may be simply that respect for persons demands that each individual must be allowed to order his life as he himself sees fit. Or it might be that control over one's own life is itself a constituent part of human well-being rather than merely a (fallible) instrument of human happiness. Or again an individual's control over his own future may be defended in terms of the beneficial effects

147

of such choice-making upon the individual himself or for the rest of society. My present concern is not with the merits of these arguments but simply to point out that they weigh against the moral effect argument as much as against straightforward paternalism.

Thus, the moral effect argument does not provide the uncomplicated alternative to paternalism that many of its proponents suppose. The difficulties that I have pointed to arise not from the ascription of duties to B but from allowing that those duties provide reason for limiting A's freedom. If someone went no further than holding that B had a duty (subject to A's consent) to help A in coping with the unfortunate consequences of his own actions, A's autonomy would remain unimpaired. Yet not to allow that duty to constitute a ground for limiting A's conduct is equally problematic for the liberal. For that would be to place B's freedom at the mercy of A's conduct. B's life would be constantly subject to the intrusions consequent upon A's reckless behaviour and that, at the very least, would seem inequitable.

This objection might itself be countered by the argument that, if a set of rules both allows individuals to engage in high-risk conduct and requires the same individuals to help others when they suffer the deleterious consequences of that conduct, then A and B enjoy neither more nor less freedom than each other. B has the same option as A to behave recklessly and A has the same duty as B to cope with the consequences. A and B therefore enjoy equal freedom and B cannot complain of being treated unfairly. However, this argument does not deal adequately with the substantive point at issue. A set of rules may itself be judged unfair if it systematically favours some modes of life at the expense of others. If the rules require those who prefer low-risk modes of life to bear the costs of those who prefer high-risk modes of life, they can be held inequitable even though, in a formal sense, they apply equally to all. Certainly, the liberal can hardly be satisfied with arrangements that enable the freedom of some to be used at the expense of the freedom of others. That is why, if the liberal ascribes duties to B, he seems also obliged to allow that they provide justification for limiting A's freedom. It is also why, in the moral effect argument, B's duty assumes a curiously hypothetical character. If A were in condition y B would have a duty to assist him, but steps should be taken to ensure that A is never in condition y so that the duty never arises.

Hence, the liberal who is not happy to allow others to stand idly by while individuals suffer the unmitigated consequences of their own actions seems caught in a dilemma. Either he ascribes duties to B but does not allow B to restrict A's freedom – in which case he violates the principle of equity. Or he accepts that B's duties justify the restriction of A's conduct – in which case he violates the right of A to be the arbiter of his own life.

★

Before considering what we are to make of this dilemma, I want to engage in a brief digression on Mill. It is not essential to my concerns in this essay to conduct yet another investigation into what Mill said, or meant to say, by way of the harm principle. However, given his authorship of that principle and his importance to liberalism more generally, it is at least worth pausing to ask where he stood on the issue of moral effect. The short answer is that, as far as I am aware, Mill never used the moral effect argument nor examined its use by others. In view of the difficulties that the argument would encounter in the context of a philosophy such as Mill's, this is perhaps as it should be. The general thrust of *On Liberty* is certainly against it. For the most part Mill writes as though it were a simple concomitant of his case for liberty that individuals must endure the full consequences of their use of that liberty. In self-regarding matters, 'there should be perfect freedom, legal and social, to do the action and stand the consequences'.[11] Moreover, in both *Utilitarianism* and *On Liberty* Mill makes clear that the most important duties individuals owe to one another are duties of restraint rather than positive duties such as would figure in a moral effect argument.[12]

Yet, in both works, he is anxious to deny that his morality is entirely negative. In part the positive duties that he identifies amount to no more than contributing one's fair share to the mutual benefits that accrue from living in society.[13] But he also recognizes as duties 'certain acts of individual beneficence, such as saving a fellow creature's life' which, since they are duties, an individual 'may rightfully be made responsible to society for not doing'.[14]

Mill's position on positive duties is complicated by his use of the distinction between duties of perfect obligation and those of imperfect obligation.[15] Duties of perfect obligation are those in virtue of which a corresponding right is held by some person or persons. Thus, not to perform such duties is to violate the rights of others and to be guilty of injustice. For Mill the spheres of perfect obligation, moral rights and justice are co-extensive. Most of the duties that he places in this sphere of morality are negative in character. But there are at least some duties to benefit others which he appears to regard as duties of perfect obligation. He seems to place the duty to save life, where it is in immediate danger, in that category.[16] This, at least, could provide a foothold for a moral effect argument. My earlier appeal to the duty to rescue a drowning man was an addition to the example of the unsafe bridge as Mill presents it in *On Liberty*; yet elsewhere he himself cites that old favourite as an obvious example of a duty.[17] If there is such a duty and some, by their conduct, risk imposing it upon others, one can begin to argue that full account should be taken of that in calculating the legitimate distribution of freedoms.

Mill is more willing to push out the boundaries of positive duty under the heading of duties of imperfect obligation.[18] He recognizes generosity and beneficence as 'duties' under that description. However, this categorization of positive duties does not automatically disarm the appeal to moral effect. Duties of imperfect obligation are still duties and we are 'bound' to practise them; we have some discretion only over when and to whom they are practised. Since they are not owed to 'assignable persons' they do not give rise to correlative rights and that, for Mill, is what distinguishes beneficence from justice. No one can claim a right to the beneficence of another. Yet Mill does not therefore consign imperfect obligations to the realm of supererogation. He does distinguish a category of acts which it is good to do and not wrong not to do, acts 'which we wish that people should do, which we like or admire them for doing, perhaps dislike or despise them for not doing, but yet admit that they are not bound to do'.[19] But those acts are not matters of imperfect obligation. Indeed, for Mill, they do not belong to the province of morality properly so-called at all, but to that of 'worthiness' or 'nobility'.[20] For Mill, morality is extensionally equivalent with the sphere of duty; he has no conceptual room for a realm of supererogation.

Imperfect obligations are then properly regarded as duties. They describe acts which it is not only right to do but also wrong not to do. Indeed, for Mill, the hallmark of any duty is that 'a person may rightfully be compelled to fulfil it'. 'Duty is a thing which may be *exacted* from a person, as one exacts a debt.'[21] Mill identifies three sorts of sanction that may be brought to bear on an individual in exacting a duty: legal penalties, social disapproval and the reproaches of the individual's own conscience. As one might expect, he seems to hold that non-legal forms of sanction are more appropriate in the case of imperfect obligations.[22] But which sanction is used would seem to be a matter of expediency rather than itself a matter of right and wrong[23] and, even if it is social censure rather than legal punishment, it is still, in Mill's eyes, coercive. Thus to be under a duty of imperfect obligation is still to be under an obligation which is morally inescapable and which, by one means or another, one may be compelled, rather than just exhorted or persuaded, to perform.

What difference does it make to the moral effect argument if the duty in question is one of imperfect obligation in Mill's sense? At first sight it may seem that there can be no such moral effect. Since there are no rights correlative to imperfect obligations, any particular A who becomes an appropriate object of beneficence cannot be said to impose an obligation upon any particular B to be his benefactor. Benefactors have no moral choice about being benefactors but they do have some choice over the occasions and the objects of their benefaction. Thus, although A may become a candidate for beneficence, B does not have to benefit A in particular and he cannot therefore claim a right to limit A's conduct on the ground that A might otherwise impose an inescapable obligation upon him.

However, moral effect cannot be dismissed so easily. The class of B persons cannot exist without the class of A persons. As long as a class of A persons exists, each individual in the class of B persons has an inescapable duty of beneficence to some, if not all, members of the A class. They may have some choice over the occasion of their performing their obligation, but, over the obligation itself and its extent, they have none. Thus the class of B persons, or any individual member of that class, can properly hold that their freedom is limited by the class of A persons so that, once again, the moral effect argument obtains a foothold. Potential B persons can claim a right to restrain potential A persons on grounds of 'self-protection'.

None of this is intended to suggest that, in some clandestine fashion, Mill subscribed to the moral effect argument. But it is meant to indicate that the issue of moral effect is present in Mill's writings even though he himself does not appear to recognize it. One can speculate about how he would have dealt with it. Perhaps he would have amended his analysis of the morality of aid and assistance. Perhaps he would have given moral significance to the distinction between distress that is the individual's own fault and that which is not. Perhaps he would have acknowledged moral effect but reckoned that it should normally weigh less in the balance of considerations than toleration. But, although we may guess at where Mill's inclinations would have taken him, the issue of moral effect remains unresolved in what he wrote.

★

Before setting off in pursuit of Mill, I had reached the conclusion that the liberal who acknowledges moral effect has problems both if he does, and if he does not, accept that effect as a reason for limiting freedom. Before looking at how that dilemma might be dealt with, let me make two points which cut the problem down to size.

Firstly, it does not follow from what I have said that the liberal runs into problems as soon as he allows that morality takes in more than negative duties. For instance, my remarks have no bearing on the issue of the initial allocation of resources amongst individuals. They concern how people should respond to what others make of their life-chances rather than what the initial distribution of life-chances should be and, therefore, constitute no objection to radical intervention to secure distributive justice. The issue of moral effect provides no grounds for an appeal from new-style to old-style liberalism. Nor does the issue of moral effect arise if B is attributed with a duty to assist A when misfortunes befall A which are not the foreseeable consequences of A's own actions. There are problems about how far one can extend the sphere of positive obligation and still leave scope for individual liberty but those are problems of a different kind.[24] There are also problems about drawing the line between what should be considered a consequence of A's action and what should not. If another earthquake were to hit San Francisco, I imagine that most of us would regard the injured as merely victims of a natural catastrophe. But the uncompromising individualist could hold that they were suffering the consequences of a risk that they knew (or could have known) they were undertaking when they chose to live in San Francisco. However, doubts about where to draw the line do not invalidate the distinction or its significance.

Secondly, there are many areas of toleration in which it is difficult to imagine moral effect arising as a serious issue. Thus, although one could contrive cases, it seems unlikely to present a problem within the general area of freedom of expression. A possible line of argument could be that C may use his freedom of expression to persuade A to act contrary to his own interests leaving B to cope with the consequences; B's interests therefore demand a limit on C's freedom of expression. However, this assumes that C, rather than A himself, is to be held responsible for A's accepting and acting on C's views and that is an assumption that the liberal is naturally reluctant to grant. Without that assumption, the moral effect of A's conduct on B cannot be used as a reason for silencing C. Freedom of religion is another area in which moral effect seems unlikely to present a serious problem.

So the issue of moral effect does not arise with every ascription of positive duty nor find its way into every area of toleration. But if the issue is limited, it is still potentially large. How should the liberal respond to the dilemma with which it confronts him?

One possibility would be to reject assertions of moral effect altogether. One might hold simply that if A's sufferings are the consequence of A's actions, B has no duty, nor any weaker moral reason, to assist A. Thus there could be no moral effect to warrant a restriction upon A's freedom. This might be described as the stance of the heroic liberal (though some might demur from the adjective 'heroic'). As I have already pointed out, it would be a mistake to identify this stance with that of negative, 'pre-revisionist', liberalism. Someone could combine the heroic stance with the most scrupulous commitment to equalizing life-chances.

153

The heroic stance has the virtues of simplicity and consistency, but does it have any others? The obvious question it poses is whether most of us could live with it. Can we really contemplate with equanimity a world in which some live in grinding poverty, are starving to death, are racked with disease and suffering terrible pain, while others, who could relieve those conditions at little cost to themselves, can nevertheless ignore those miseries without compunction simply because they are the outcomes of the sufferers' own actions?

The heroic stance would be slightly modified if it were held that it would be virtuous of B to assist A even though it would not be wrong of him not to offer assistance. In other words, moral effect would be acknowledged but only to the extent of supererogation. That too would be consistent with leaving A's freedom un-impaired. But if B's assistance were no more than a matter of supererogation, B could not be subject to moral criticism if he failed to assist A. That invites the same rhetorical response as I have just given to the unmodified heroic stance.

Could the proponent of toleration ascribe duties to B without accepting those as reasons for limiting A's freedom? I have already indicated the charge of inequity that this response is likely to encounter. However, there are cases in which that objection either does not arise or may be circumvented. Firstly, there are many cases in which A and B would turn out to be the same person. That is, those who take the risks are virtually identical with those who are liable to incur the duties. Just carrying on the ordinary business of life involves risks. Strictly speaking these may not be 'un-avoidable' but their avoidance would require an abnormal form of life. Ordinarily, we would wish to be helped by others if we fell victim to these common hazards of life just as we would feel obliged to help others in those circumstances. Where there is this simple identity between the takers of risks and the bearers of duties, the problem of equity does not arise. All that needs to be deter-mined is the mutually acceptable balance of risks and duties.

Secondly there are cases in which the objection of inequity arises but may be satisfactorily disposed of. Suppose a risk is unique to an individual but some benefit redounds to others from his taking that risk. That benefit may then make it worth their while tolerating the risky activity even though they may be saddled with a duty if something goes wrong. Mill's argument for experiments in living could be viewed in this light. If such experiments really do have a high social value, it might be good policy to encourage people to experiment by cushioning them from the full effects of the risks that they take. This may not be the most persuasive of examples. An obligation to support indiscriminate experiments in living hardly seems a persuasive plea and the notion of 'experiments' in living is rather odd if nothing can ever be learned from the results and we have to allow the same experiments to be repeated without limit. However it does at least illustrate a *form* of argument that may be acceptable.

A third way of attempting to meet the charge of inequity is more controversial. Suppose that the benefit of the freedom to A is greater than the burden of the duty to B. The simple utilitarian response would then be that A should have his freedom and B endure his duty. This response does not so much rebut the charge of inequity as ignore it. Even if the utility A obtains from the risk outweighs the disutility B incurs from the duty, B can still quite properly object that his interests are being subordinated to those of A. That A should be able to use his freedom at the expense of B remains unfair however small the disadvantage to B.

Finally, the liberal who accepts that, when A's actions have adverse consequences for A, they may also have moral consequences for B, may also accept that that justifies a limit upon A's freedom. In other words, he may find the full-blooded moral effect argument more acceptable than the other alternatives on some, if not all, occasions. I have shown that the moral effect argument involves others imposing their concept of what is good for A upon A and that unwelcome implication has therefore to be swallowed by the liberal who opts for this alternative. The nature of the presumption of what is for A's good then becomes crucial. Other things being equal, a moral effect argument will be more or less acceptable depending upon the more or less acceptable character of the self-regarding presumption that it entails. For example, an intervention to prevent A from behaving recklessly will be easier to accept if it can be established, with reasonable certainty, that A is disposed to behave in that way only because he is misinformed or under-informed about the likely consequences of his actions. Were he possessed of the relevant information, he himself would choose not to behave in that way.[25] The issue of moral effect thus resolves partly, though not wholly, into the much-discussed question of more or less acceptable forms of paternalism. The liberal will then have to find solace in the fact that he can still resort to his principles in discriminating amongst paternalistic claims and thereby keep appeals to moral effect within bounds.

Notes

This paper was presented to a conference on toleration at the University of York supported by the Morrell Trust and has benefited greatly from the comments and criticisms of those who participated in the seminar.

1 J. S. Mill, *On Liberty*, in *Utilitarianism, Liberty and Considerations on Representative Government*, ed. H. B. Acton, London, 1910, 73.

2 ibid., 132. Cf. also p. 150: 'it must by no means be supposed, because damage, or probability of damage, to the interests of others, can alone justify the interference of society, that therefore it always does justify such interference.'

3 ibid., 151–2.

4 F. A. von Hayek, *The Constitution of Liberty*, London, 1966, 286.

5 Milton Friedman, *Capitalism and Freedom*, Chicago, 1962, 188. See also Joel Feinberg, 'Legal paternalism', *Canadian Journal of Philosophy*, 1, 1971, 119. For examples of judicial use of the public charge argument in the United States, see Terry S. Kogan, 'The limits of state intervention: personal identity and ultra-risky actions', *Yale Law Journal*, 85, 1976, 832–3.

6 Hayek also seems inclined to speak of the duty in question as one of 'charity'; see op. cit., 292.

7 *On Liberty*, 73.

8 Not only does the best-judge principle run counter to everyday experience, it also runs into some logical difficulties. Suppose A, B and C each want to achieve the same end but pursue different strategies for attaining it. Each might, for example, want to maximize his return on an investment but each invest in a different company. B's investment proves more successful than A's or C's. If this is more than a matter of luck, we seem obliged to concede,

not only that B was a better judge of his own interest than either
A or C but also that B was a better judge of A's and C's interests
than were they themselves. Suppose now that A and B each want
to attain different ends, y and z respectively. Why should each be
an inferior judge of the best mode of attaining the other's end simply
because he does not want to attain it? Would some magical epistemic
change occur if A and B subsequently changed preferences so that
A wanted z and B wanted y? Moreover, the very assertion that
others are the best judges of their own interests involves something
of a paradox. How can B judge that A is the best judge of A's interest
without B himself being at least as good a judge of A's interest and
therefore in a position to judge A's judgement?

9   e.g. Rolf E. Sartorius, *Individual Conduct and Social Norms*, Belmont,
California, 1975, 154–6.

10   *On Liberty*, 140.

11   ibid., 132.

12   J. S. Mill, *Utilitarianism*, in *Utilitarianism, Liberty and Considerations
on Representative Government*, ed. H. B. Acton, London, 1910, 55–6;
On Liberty, 74.

13   *On Liberty*, 74, 132.

14   ibid., 74.

15   *Utilitarianism*, 46–7.

16   ibid., 59; *On Liberty*, 74.

17   *Utilitarianism*, 17. Presumably this has to count as a duty of perfect
obligation since, if A is in the river and cannot swim and B is on
the river bank and can swim, B has a duty to an 'assignable' person.

18   ibid., 46–7.

19   ibid., 45.

20   ibid., 46.

21   ibid., 45.

22   *On Liberty*, 74, 132.

23   *Utilitarianism*, 44.

24   See James S. Fishkin, *The Limits of Obligation*, London, 1982.

25   For examples of attempts to chart an area of justified paternalism
along these lines see J. Feinberg, op. cit., Gerald Dworkin, 'Paternalism', *The Monist*, 56, 1972 and Rosemary Carter, 'Justifying
paternalism', *Canadian Journal of Philosophy*, 7, 1977.

8

Toleration as a moral ideal

PETER P. NICHOLSON

Introduction

In surveying a recent debate on toleration, I have been struck by two major divergences.[1] First, some seek a morally neutral description, whilst others treat toleration as a moral ideal. Second, some see it as needing strong justification and justifiable only as the lesser of two evils, whereas for others it is either intrinsically good itself or else inseparable from something that is. Clearly, these are deep disagreements. I do not expect to resolve them. My aim is to examine the familiar ideal of toleration which is widely acknowledged in our society, however partially it is realized in practice, and by spelling out its assumptions and implications to offer a fuller account. Simultaneously I defend the thesis that though there are two distinct sides to toleration, they are necessarily connected – there are not 'two concepts of toleration'. It is important to be explicit about this because my analysis of toleration produces precisely the ingredients from which one is tempted to construct a divide between negative and positive concepts of toleration to parallel the division between negative and positive concepts of freedom. I think that the distinction between negative and positive freedoms is mistaken, distorts especially the understanding of positive freedom, and misdirects the search for the true unity of freedom: but I do not wish to argue that now. I do wish to argue, however, that there are not two concepts of toleration. I contend that toleration, understood as a moral ideal, has both a negative side, much discussed, and a positive side, far

TOLERATION AS A MORAL IDEAL

less discussed – and that its full moral force is grasped only when the two sides are taken together.

Terminology

English possesses three words: 'toleration', 'tolerance' and 'tolerationism'. Some writers have attempted to distinguish between them so that they refer to different aspects of toleration. I find no agreement over usage, and no suggestion which is relevant within the area I am considering. Crick, for instance, proposes 'tolerance' for the act or practice of being tolerant, and 'toleration' for the explicit doctrine that one should be tolerant; noting that historically there was 'tolerance' before there was 'toleration'. I think, however, that in ordinary usage 'toleration' means precisely the act of being tolerant (or the disposition to be tolerant), and that it is easily distinguished from a doctrine of toleration without introducing a further term. Moreover, if a further term is to be used 'tolerationism' seems more appropriate, as Raphael observes.

I stick to 'toleration' and its forms 'tolerate', 'tolerant', and 'tolerator', and do not use 'tolerance'. *The Oxford English Dictionary*'s lists of meanings of 'toleration' and 'tolerance' overlap in some instances. Where they differ, my concern is with toleration and not with tolerance. Thus Raphael writes that 'tolerance' is 'more common ... when one wants to speak of purely physical or passive endurance or resistance' (a distinction King notes too, and thinks can be ignored). But what I shall discuss has nothing to do with passive endurance. Again, Crick often uses 'tolerance' to refer to society's capacity to sustain dissent: this usage is consciously modelled on the *OED*'s technical meaning of 'tolerance' as 'an allowable amount of variation' in the weight or fineness of a coin or in the dimensions of a machine or part. The idea, I take it, is that just as a machine with a piston which is too loose will not function, neither can a society which allows excessive departures from its norms and practices survive as a society. There are, of course, very interesting questions about tolerance, about how much dissent or faction or conflict societies can in fact tolerate (endure); but these involve sociological matters beyond the scope of this essay.

Toleration can be practised either by individuals or by groups

159

of individuals. Men and women can be tolerant or not in their private lives: and at the public level, so too can societies, other social groupings, governments, and states. I limit the discussion to the case of political toleration, that is, toleration by governments and states, exercised through constitutions, statutes, regulations and policies, with respect to the opinions and actions of individuals and groups within their jurisdiction or power.

A definition

How, then, is 'toleration', considered as a moral ideal, to be defined? The following, most of them commonly mentioned in analyses of toleration, are its constituents:

1 *Deviance*. What is tolerated deviates from what the tolerator thinks, or does, or believes should be done.
2 *Importance*. The subject of the deviation is not trivial.
3 *Disapproval*. The tolerator disapproves morally of the deviation.
4 *Power*. The tolerator has the power to try to suppress or prevent (or at least to oppose or hinder) what is tolerated.
5 *Non-rejection*. None the less, the tolerator does not exercise his power, thereby allowing the deviation to continue. (I prefer 'non-rejection' to the more usual 'acceptance'.)
6 *Goodness*. Toleration is right and the tolerator is good.

Several of these need expansion. Sometimes 'dislike' is added to 'disapproval', the latter being understood as resting upon moral reasons and the former as being non-moral and non-rational feeling; for instance, Cranston argues that unless we include 'dislike' we cut out such matters as racial prejudice. The addition of 'dislike' may well be important for the historical or sociological study of toleration, where 'toleration' is a descriptive term. A definition of the moral ideal, however, must exclude 'dislike'. Raphael correctly stresses that we must see the moral ideal of toleration solely in terms of disapproval, i.e. of the making of judgements and the holding of reasons over which moral argument is possible. Toleration is a matter of moral choice, and our tastes or inclinations are irrelevant. No doubt people's prejudices, their contingent feelings of liking or disliking, have to be taken into account when one is trying to explain why they are tolerant or not; but such feelings are not morally grounded, and cannot be the ground of a moral position.

It is widely agreed that power is a necessary condition of the exercise of toleration. Of course, a powerless person could be tolerant in the sense of being of a tolerant disposition or believing in toleration, if he would exercise toleration were he to have the power. In politics, in fact, everyone does have at least some power. Even if the government has decreed that a particular opinion or action be tolerated or not tolerated, it is within every citizen's power to decide whether he will enthusiastically uphold and support that law or deliberately evade and thwart it. He can, within limits, be intolerant where the law has commanded him to be tolerant, and tolerant where it has ordered intolerance; and if enough citizens refuse to accept and apply the law, the authorities' power can be greatly reduced. Power, and hence the possibility of toleration, is widely dispersed between governments and subjects. This does not, however, affect the basic point that power is a precondition to choosing non-rejection. A corollary is that strictly speaking there cannot be toleration of opinions or the holding of opinions, only of the expression of opinions, since the latter alone is within other people's power to reject or not.

The sixth constituent – which is the most contentious – is complicated too. 'Toleration' is part of our moral vocabulary. It is not only a moral concept in the sense that it is applicable to moral action, like for example 'responsibility', but also in the narrower sense that, like 'courage', it is a virtue. Toleration as a moral ideal cannot be value-neutral, and for this reason too it must be distinguished from the descriptive concept of toleration which can and should be value-neutral. King, and Crick too at times, define toleration and intolerance descriptively and say they are 'in themselves neither good or bad', meaning that people can tolerate what they should be intolerant of and fail to tolerate what they should be tolerant of. Lukes qualifies this on the ground that since what is being described is a value, the descriptive concept of toleration cannot be free of all values. The tolerator is claiming that his disapproval is morally justified and that he has a right to act on it if he wishes: he does not merely possess power but also the authority to exercise it. Furthermore, Lukes argues, to characterize

someone as tolerant would normally be understood to endorse his
right to give orders. Even on Lukes's view, however, 'toleration'
is a descriptive or sociological concept. His account connects the
values a person holds with what he tolerates, but it remains value-
neutral because it regards all values as equally legitimate. The
moral beliefs and corresponding toleration depend upon con-
textually given norms. Differences between values and over what
should be tolerated are to be explained sociologically, not judged.
I am not disputing the merits of Lukes's view. I introduce his
account in order to discriminate between the descriptive concept
and the moral concept of toleration. Two differences are worth
emphasizing. First, whereas for Lukes what is morally right depends on the social context, the moral ideal raises the further
question whether the moral beliefs in a society or section of society
are right. Second, whereas on Lukes's view there is a right not to
be tolerant, which the tolerator waives, and hence no right to be
tolerated, according to the moral ideal toleration is a duty, there
is no right not to be tolerant, and there can be a right to be
tolerated.

To sum up: toleration is the virtue of refraining from exercising
one's power to interfere with others' opinion or action although
that deviates from one's own over something important and
although one morally disapproves of it. The opposite of toleration
is intolerance. That might seem too obvious to state: but Crick for
example writes that the opposite of toleration is indifference and
the opposite of intolerance is full acceptance. Now it is true that
where there is indifference or acceptance the question of toleration
does not arise. Conditions 2 or 3, or both, are not met. None the
less, when the conditions are met, intolerance is the opposite
response from toleration: it is the vice of exercising one's power
to interfere with opinions or actions which deviate from one's own
and of which one morally disapproves.

The central feature of my account is the claim that toleration
is good. Not everyone agrees. Some think that toleration may be
good or it may not, depending on the circumstances; whilst those
who think it is good – whether always or in some cases – disagree
on why it is good. The next section looks at one line of reasoning
about the goodness of toleration. Essentially, it presents the case
against not being tolerant. Toleration is preferable because of the

weight of the reasons against intolerance. Accordingly, I call this the negative case for toleration: it is the negative side of toleration. Thereafter the positive case for toleration is presented, which gives reasons directly for toleration itself. An attempt is then made to show how the two cases for toleration must be taken together, by discussing the question of whether being tolerant reduces one's freedom or not. Finally, I examine the limits of toleration.

The negative case for toleration

The tolerator is faced by an opinion or action which he thinks is wrong. Not only does he repudiate it for himself, he also believes that it is wrong for anyone else to hold this opinion or behave in this way. Since the opinion or action is wrong, there is a presumption that it would be right to suppress the one or prevent the other, and stop wrong ideas being communicated or wrong being done. What are the arguments for refraining, and being tolerant? The following negative reasons are frequently offered.

First, it may be too expensive, in material costs or moral values, to end the wrong. Persecution of religions or political ideologies may disrupt the economy and destabilize the political system. Laws making certain sexual acts or drug-taking into criminal offences cannot be enforced without considerable inroads into privacy. Eradicating the evil of prostitution may promote greater sexual violence against women, which is worse. If people are prevented from providing goods which are in heavy demand, such as alcohol or pornography, there is a danger that others will step in to meet the demand illegitimately, and organized crime be encouraged. A system of control must give some person or body the power to decide what to tolerate and what not, thereby risking mistakes, incompetence, and abuse of power.

Second, in practice it may prove very difficult to extirpate the opinion or stop the action. If that is the objective, then the more effective method may be to tolerate them whilst campaigning against them. Instead of driving them underground, where they may persist unknown or may flourish on notoriety, it may be better to confront them openly and persuade people that that opinion should be rejected and the action forgone.

Third, it may be argued that beliefs and motives are beyond the

163

law's reach anyway. Governments can force people to profess a belief but not to accept it or to give up their real belief, and can force them to act in a particular way but not to do it for the right motive.

Thus, following the negative line of reasoning, not to be tolerant is exhibited as too costly, as ineffective, and as simply impossible beyond a certain point. Finally, the whole matter can be turned around and it can be asked: if the opinions or actions in question are not socially injurious what reason is there *not* to tolerate them?

Looking at the matter from the negative side, toleration is doing what you do not want to, namely allow wrong opinions and actions to continue, because you want intolerance even less. From this side, toleration is indeed the ordering of priorities, as King suggests, a prudential calculation (Barber), 'a makeshift, suitable for an overcrowded and overheated planet' (Forster).[2] To take two of King's examples, one may tolerate an objectionable religion in one's own country in order to set an example for the toleration of one's own religion elsewhere, or one may tolerate communists because too many fundamental and potentially dangerous constitutional adjustments would be required to eliminate them. But on this view, one's priorities are, so to say, imposed on one: and were they otherwise, and one could eliminate the objectionable religion or the communists without the undesirable side-effects, then one would stamp them out. Likewise, one would not have to tolerate the opinions and actions of any minority which was sufficiently easily identified, small, economically inessential and powerless. Yet there is, of course, far more to toleration than this. What that is, emerges when we turn to the positive case.

The positive case for toleration

The positive side of toleration involves a different perspective. If toleration is good, and there are positive reasons for it, we need not think of it as our doing what we do not want to do. In what way then, can it be argued that toleration is good? There are two sets of reasons, depending on whether toleration is regarded as an instrumental good or a constituent in some wider good on the one hand, or on the other hand an intrinsic good itself.

On the first view, toleration is good because it is a necessary means to or condition of an intrinsic good, or a constituent of a good. This intrinsic good may be freedom, or justice, or civilization, or truth, or some combination of them. For instance, Raphael writes that toleration has a positive value because it contributes to liberty. He advocates toleration because it allows liberty, and advocates liberty because it enables people to do what they choose for themselves to do. Again, Rawls treats toleration as part of justice, so that the principles of justice provide a case for toleration. Everyone has an equal right to toleration: no one can claim it for his own opinions and actions, and in fairness deny its extension to everybody else.[3] Others, J. S. Mill for example, argue for toleration because they believe it is necessary for human progress and the advance of civilization, both technological and moral. Each of these positions takes a positive view of toleration because it provides reasons directly in favour of toleration. They have the limitation, however, that they reduce toleration to an instance or species of another value. They fail to consider it as a separate moral ideal and to appreciate its distinctive moral contribution.

A stronger positive case is found in the second view, where toleration is a distinct good. By being required to take heed of the ideas of others, whether simply as opinions or as embodied in their lifestyles, and above all when one forces oneself to do so, one is schooled and educated. One is shown that part of being moral, and of treating other moral agents morally, is to give serious consideration to their ideas; not to do that, whilst claiming it for one's own ideas, is not simply selfishness or the illegitimate demand for a privileged position, it is in a profound sense immorality, failure to respect human personality. Again, one is having pointed out a duty to understand ideas which may be alien and unpalatable, even evil, but which have a valid claim to our attention because they too are the deeply held convictions of human beings. The moral ideal of toleration does not require the tolerator to acknowledge any merit in the opinions of which he disapproves; but he must respect the personality of the holders of those opinions, and treat them as rational moral agents whose views can be discussed and disputed, and who are capable of changing their minds on rational grounds. Of course, a consequence of taking this attitude might be that he is encouraged to probe his own ideas, and attain a better grasp of their full meaning and implications; which may lead to some development in them, or even to the modification or rejection of some of them – or to their reinforcement. That, however, would be a side-effect and independent of toleration's intrinsic moral worth.

Looking from the positive side, and especially from the second version of it, it becomes clear that toleration is good in itself. We can be tolerant not because we cannot really avoid it, but because we think it is right and desirable. Rather than being driven to toleration, we should deliberately seek it out. Toleration is not a second best, a necessary evil, a putting up with what we have to for the sake of peace and quiet, but a positive good, a virtue distinctive of the best people and the best societies.

Toleration and freedom

As I said at the beginning, I do not want to argue that the two sides of toleration are two distinct, separate concepts of toleration, which are opposed to one another, and between which one can choose. My presentation so far may have encouraged that interpretation; so it is time to explain why I think that although the positive side of toleration is in several ways the opposite of the negative, none the less the two are complementary, so that the moral ideal of toleration must be understood as the unity of the two sides. I hope to show this by asking whether or not being tolerant reduces one's freedom.

At first glance, toleration involves a loss of freedom. The tolerator, by definition, was free to put into effect his disapproval, and by deciding not to exercise his power he has relinquished that freedom. Yet several qualifications need to be made. In most cases, he still has the option of ceasing to tolerate by exercising his power later (one exception is discussed on page 169). The tolerator may even have the legal right not to be tolerant, so that he is in the position of waiving his right and granting a permission which he may withdraw later. In this sense he remains as free as before. Considered from the moral point of view, his position is different yet ultimately the same. Since toleration is good, to be tolerant is a duty (to oneself alone, or to others too), and therefore the tolerator has no moral right not to be tolerant. He is not free to withdraw his toleration. But this does not mean that he is less free by being tolerant, simply that morally speaking one is not free in the first place; toleration is a duty and the question of being free to tolerate or not does not arise.

Another qualification is that when a person consents to being tolerant, he does not restrict his freedom. That is, the government which makes the tolerant laws or regulations, those who consent to that government and to its actions, and those who accept the justice of the laws and regulations, are all imposing upon themselves the relevant restrictions upon their exercise of power. What counts here, I think, is that the moral ideal of toleration makes it rational that a person should freely consent to being tolerant. He need not be in the situation of Hobbes's vanquished 'consenting' to the rule of their conqueror, accepting toleration because they can discover no better alternative; he can consent to toleration because he believes it is something good, which he actively wants.

This brings me to the final qualification, that the person who freely consents to toleration, and who understands the way in which it is a moral good, that is who can see it from the positive side, realizes that his freedom has been increased. Moreover, he realizes that it has not been increased at the cost of a reduction of some original freedom, which he has forgone. He is not trading off some 'new' freedom to test his ideas against those of others for his 'old' freedom to suppress those ideas. For imposing restrictions on himself is a necessary part of being tolerant and is therefore a constituent part of his freedom. This may sound like double-talk which is undesirable obscurity or mystification, so let me add another example. In presenting a paper at a seminar a person accepts certain restrictions on his behaviour, since he is agreeing to be governed by conventions about politeness, about what counts as a relevant or acceptable or good argument, about allowing others to speak, about listening and following what they say, and so on. In order to obtain a discussion of his paper he has to accept procedural rules of order. Clearly these do not limit his freedom. For what he wants is ordered discussion; not for everyone – not even for himself alone – to be able to say what they like when they like. That would not be freedom. He wants to have

167

ordered discussion: restrictions, on himself as well as others, are constitutive of his freedom. This line of argument applies even more obviously to more general questions about freedom and law or the state where it is patent that the ideal of 'freedom' outside of or independent of the law or state is simply chimerical. Likewise, the idea of a society without toleration is, morally speaking, nonsensical.

At the same time I readily concede, since it is implied in the above, that when anyone is forced to be tolerant, then his freedom is reduced. He cannot be 'forced to be free', he can only be forced to let others be free. He can be forced to be negatively tolerant, but he cannot be forced to be positively tolerant, for that is beyond the power of government or of any other individual – it is in his own power alone. On the other hand, where the moral ideal of toleration is practised, the person unwillingly being negatively tolerant will himself be treated with positive toleration by others who will note his dissent from toleration, and will set out to bring home to him the merits of toleration. If they succeed, he will have been helped to free himself.

Thus a great deal turns on the question whether or not we are to think of there being two concepts of toleration. If it were held that there are two concepts, one modelled on the negative case and the other on the positive, then it would be even harder to grasp the unity of the two sides than it already is. One would tend to regard the 'negative concept of toleration' as real toleration, and the 'positive concept' as somehow a different thing altogether, perhaps a distinct value (say self-development), which supplied a use to which (negative) toleration might be put and which would give it worth. Any such reduction of toleration to its negative side would displace the moral ideal of toleration altogether. If, on the other hand, we are prepared to entertain the thought that toleration is a single moral concept with a negative and a positive side, then I believe we can begin to get to grips with toleration as a whole. We may be able to appreciate the truth in such an apparently paradoxical statement as 'toleration is freedom'. For toleration contributes to freedom not simply because the person tolerated is freed, but also because the tolerator, far from giving up any freedom, gains it too. When the tolerator consents to the toleration freely and with adequate understanding of what he is doing, he is not restricting his own freedom of action but making a moral choice which is a constituent in a free life.

The limits of toleration

Toleration sets its own limits, as must any moral ideal. For every ideal includes some moral principle or assumption which is part of its justification and which rules out some things as unjustified and unprotected by the ideal because outside its field. Thus the moral ideal of toleration does not require us to put up with everything whatever it is. Instead the ideal stipulates two major limits. First we should reject whatever contravenes the moral base on which the ideal of toleration rests, namely, respect for all persons as full moral agents. We are not, for instance, obliged to take no action when someone speaks defamatorily or assaults a person: these are violations of individuals' legitimate rights and do not belong to the class of expression and action covered by the moral ideal of toleration – the question of toleration just does not arise here. The second major limit, which is a special case of the first, is that we should reject whatever contravenes the ideal of toleration itself. The suggestion that one ought to tolerate the destruction of toleration is, quite simply, self-contradictory.

It is, of course, very hard to specify the boundaries of toleration and locate precisely the limits to it. I think that any and every expression of opinion ought to be tolerated, including the advocacy of intolerance. The arguments in favour of toleration which can be given from the positive side seem to me to apply with equal force to all opinions. The crucial practical problem is to be able to distinguish between the expression of opinions, which must always be tolerated, and the acting out of opinions, which need not always be tolerated. Callinicos provides troublesome instances, the racialists and fascists in contemporary Britain. Perhaps the most difficult judgement of all is to know when one has reached 'the point of no return' beyond which one will no longer have the opportunity to change from a policy of toleration because one will have lost the power to do so (the exception referred to on page 166).

No moral ideal can be expected to contain answers to the problems of its practical application. Yet it must be acknowledged that the extent of those problems is very great. Part of taking seriously the opinions of which one disapproves is the acceptance that they might spread and, if put into practice, challenge and undermine institutions and values one holds dear. But the mere possibility does not justify intolerance of the expression of opinions. Furthermore, by securing the free expression of obnoxious and even intolerant opinion the tolerator upholds and reinforces his own values, demonstrating how highly he rates toleration and the morality it rests upon. Conversely, government intolerance can deal a more serious blow to that morality than can the actions of an intolerant minority.

It must also be remembered that toleration does not mean we lack commitment to our own ideals, or are surrendering them. We are enjoined not to suppress ideas of which we disapprove: we are not being asked to like or support or encourage them. All that toleration requires is, negatively, that we permit the free expression of ideas we disapprove of and, positively, that we agree to the moral value of there being free expression of ideas we disapprove of. This rules out censorship, but still leaves us room to censure and to counter in various ways ideas from which we dissent. Indeed, the moral ideal of toleration presupposes that we will do exactly that. To take a current example, on this view of toleration a government may not curb free expression of racialist opinions (the 1976 Race Relations Act includes such a curb, if only a minor one). But that does not mean that the government should do nothing. Governments have available to them many ways of pursuing an equivalent of the disinterested support of right ideas which Mill urged upon individuals.[4] A government can discriminate against one idea by giving extra aid to the opposite idea, which it does approve, for instance by policies of reverse discrimination favouring minority racial groups.[5] A government can also take steps to dissuade those who hold racialist views and to furnish them instead with convictions which are wiser and more elevated; and in doing so it may even obtrude its own opinion and exhortations upon the individual. But the government may not proceed beyond persuasion: the final judge between opinions must be the individual. For example, no office should be closed to him because of his opinions, for the sole relevant criterion is his ability to discharge its duties efficiently and loyally. Cromwell stated it correctly: 'the State in choosing men to serve them [sc. the public] takes no notice of their opinions; if they be willing faithfully to serve them, that suffices'.[6]

It may be argued further that the tolerator need not provide the same protection he would for ideas and practices he did morally approve of. For instance Bakunin, in one of his moments of undiluted libertarianism, argued that after the revolution all adults must be absolutely free, *inter alia*, to voice all opinions, and to organize associations even for immoral purposes (e.g. to exploit or corrupt the naive or alcoholic, or to worship God) and even for the purpose of advocating the destruction of individual and public freedom. Bakunin is content to let public discussion expose charlatans and pernicious associations, laying down the single condition that society must refuse to guarantee the civil rights of any association whose aims or rules are unjust. Thus an association advocating the end of toleration would be 'juridically unrecognised', so that for example agreements with it would not be binding and it would not be able to sue its debtors.[7] The intolerant and the unjust are not prohibited from holding or advocating their ideas, but neither is any legal support or sanction or mark of recognition accorded to them. Every adult member of society is treated as a full moral agent. All are free to advocate, and to adopt, any opinion: if any allow themselves to be deluded or exploited then that is their own responsibility. Different assumptions, by contrast, are made by those who wish to suppress the expression of immoral opinions. To advocate the suppression of racialist or sexist opinions, for instance, on the ground that their free expression will help them to spread, thereby bolstering unjust institutions, exhibits a low opinion of other members of one's society. It supposes that some will be converted to these ideas, either because they are predisposed to them and to injustice, or because they are not alert or intelligent enough to grasp all that accepting the ideas involves: and at the same time it supposes that the advocate of suppression has a superior insight into what is unjust and a greater resistance to injustice. Such assumptions are very troublesome for the adherent to the moral ideal of toleration. He is committed to treating every person as a moral agent, and to allowing every person the opportunity to practise the virtue of toleration – even though this entails allowing scope for the vice of intolerance. At the same time, he must admit that severe practical difficulties surround his ideal, and that sometimes the conditions necessary for its successful practice are partially or entirely missing. Some people may be so fixed in their own ideas that they are unable to contemplate extending any genuine consideration to opinions they disapprove of, and unable to treat the holders of those opinions as moral equals. Again, a society may contain a significant minority, even a majority, which is fully committed to intolerance and which repudiates the morality behind the ideal of toleration. In these circumstances, would a government necessarily be wrong if it decided that it was too dangerous and irresponsible not to temper or ration its toleration or supply it selectively? It would be absurd to deny that such circumstances occur, and presumptuous to think that any statement of a moral ideal could resolve such political problems. None the less, the moral ideal of toleration remains relevant and important because it highlights crucial moral features of the practical issues. Toleration permits limitation of itself when that is necessary in order to protect the moral values which justify it. The moral goal, however, remains the removal of those limits and the widest possible extension of toleration. When a government is unable to practise the virtue of toleration to the full, it should admit its failure, identify its source (e.g. that the society contains too many people who cannot be trusted to behave responsibly), and set out to remedy it. Above all, the moral ideal of toleration assumes that everyone is capable of being morally responsible. Consequently, it opposes any permanent paternalism which assumes that some members of society can never become tolerant, for that assumption is incompatible with the moral reasoning implicit in the positive side of toleration.

Notes

1 The debate is in *Government and Opposition*, 6, 1971. Major papers are contributed by Bernard Crick on 'Toleration and tolerance in theory and practice' and by Preston King on 'The problem of tolerance'. These are followed by shorter comments and contribu-

tions: Maurice Cranston, 'Crick on toleration'; Ernest Gellner, 'The dangers of tolerance'; Peter Laslett, 'Political theory and political science research'; Steven Lukes, 'Social and moral tolerance'; D. D. Raphael, 'Toleration, choice and liberty'; and Alan Ryan, 'The open society and utility'. Crick reprints his paper in his collection *Political Theory and Practice*, London, 1972, and King incorporates his in the first chapter of his book *Toleration*, London, 1976. Since I seldom refer to these studies, and then usually to express disagreement, let me make it clear that I have profited from reading them, and not hesitated to draw from them.

2 Benjamin R. Barber, *Superman and Common Men: Freedom, Anarchy and the Revolution*, Harmondsworth, 1972, ch. 4; E. M. Forster, 'Tolerance', in *Two Cheers for Democracy*, London, 1951.

3 John Rawls, *A Theory of Justice*, Oxford, 1972, sect. 34.

4 J. S. Mill, *On Liberty*, London, 1859, near the beginning of ch. IV.

5 See Lord Scarman's plea for legal measures positively to protect and favour racial and other minorities in his J. B. and W. B. Morrell Memorial Lecture of 1983, *Toleration and the Law*, York.

6 Quoted by B. Crick, op. cit.

7 Michael Bakunin, 'Revolutionary catechism' (1866), in *Bakunin on Anarchy*, ed. S. Dolgoff, Montreal, 1980, 79–80 and 82.

Index

harms – *cont.*
private or individual, 130;
public or social, 130–1
Hart, H. L. A., 5
Hayek, F. A. von, 139, 140
Hegel, G. W. F., 44
Hobbes, T., 43, 167
homosexuality, 5, 7–8, 19
Horkheimer, M. 58

indecency, 81, 93, 100, 106
individual, the: and society,
16–18, 58–60, 62, 64; and
the state, 3–4
interests, 125–9; best-judge
principle, 21, 23, 147; and
harm, 22–3, 144
intolerance, 11, 120, 161,
162–3, 169–70, 171–2; in
Marcuse, 53, 59, 61–7

Kafka, Franz, 120
King, Preston, 159, 161, 164
King-Hamilton, Mr Justice,
78
Kirkup, James, 9, 79, 88, 92,
95
Knuller v. *DPP*, 102

law, 8, 17, 18, 113, 116; and
enforcement of morality,
5–6, 111; natural, 37–40,
42–3; *for specific laws see
under titles*
Lemon, Denis, 9, 79
Letter on Toleration, A, 2, 3
liberalism, 4, 5–6, 59, 71; and
concept of harm, 12,
116–17, 132–3; and moral

effect, 142, 144, 147–9,
152–6
liberty, *see* freedom
limits of toleration, 13, 53, 59,
61–7, 67–72, 136, 169–72
Locke, John, 36–9, 40–3, 48,
105; conception of
freedom, 37–9, 41–3, 47–8;
A Letter on Toleration, 2, 3;
*Two Treatises of
Government*, 36–9, 41–3, 48
Lucas, J. R., 118–25, 130
Lukes, Steven, 161–2

MacIntyre, Alasdair, 54, 61–2,
63–4, 66
Malcolm, Derek, 117
Marcuse, Herbert, 53–67, 70;
An Essay on Liberation, 60,
63–4, 65, 66; *One-
Dimensional Man*, 58–9, 62,
63, 66; 'Repressive
Tolerance', 53, 55–63, 64–7
Marx, Karl, 66
Mill, John Stuart, 14, 22, 53,
147, 165, 170; defence of
freedom of expression, 4,
6–7, 57; duties,
identification of, 149–51;
'experiments in living', 19,
20, 155; harm principle,
3–5, 11–12, 113–17, 136–7,
142, 144; *On Liberty*, 1,
3–7, 19–20, 47, 57, 70,
113–17, 149–51; Marcuse's
critique of, 58, 64; and
moral effect, 149–52; self-
regarding/other-regarding
distinction, 4–6, 114; *System*